Tarawa: a legend is born

Henry I Shaw

BB

Editor-in-Chief: Barrie Pitt
Art Director: Peter Dunbar

Military Consultant: Sir Basil Liddell Hart
Picture Editor: Robert Hunt

Executive Editor: David Mason
Designer: John Marsh
Cover: Denis Piper
Research Assistant: Yvonne Marsh
Cartographer: Richard Natkiel
Special Drawings: John Batchelor

Contents

The lessons of amphibious warfare

Introduction by Barrie Pitt

Despite a distinguished history lasting nearly 170 years, the United States Marine Corps had, in 1943, no experience of major amphibious landings against strongly defended enemy territory. They had previously served mainly as landing troops in naval operations, or as boarding parties, or as guards for naval stations. But in the Second World War the scope of the fighting, and the geographical characteristics of enemy held territories, called for a new task to be fulfilled.

General Marshall summed up the changed circumstances when he said in 1943: 'My military education and experience in the First World War has all been based on roads, rivers, and railroads. During the last two years, however, I have been acquiring an education based on oceans and I've had to learn all over again. Prior to the present war I never heard of any landing-craft except a rubber boat. Now I think about little else.'

In the years between the wars, the doctrines and techniques of amphibious assault were worked out by leading Marines, often at variance with established ideas, and the men went through the motions of training. Then came the need for the techniques to be tried in an actual landing, and the small atoll of Tarawa in the Gilbert Islands suddenly took on a new and important role.

It was not the only amphibious assault by any means. The Solomons, New Britain and New Guinea all saw such landings, but they were opposed only lightly, or indeed not at all.

The Tarawa invasion, however, was the first to be carried out directly against heavily defended beaches, and here the theory and training of the prewar years was put to the critical test.

Tarawa was, of course, not only a sounding board for the strategists' ideas. Its proponents would have been little thanked for the loss of so many men if it had been no more than a field experiment. Though its value was subsequently disputed by at least one of the commanders who took part, the atoll was considered essential as a base for operations in the Marshall Islands, as its airfields provided land bases for extensive bombing runs, as well as strafing runs by fighters against Japanese installations and shipping. Equally, it became possible to carry out from these airfields systematic photo-reconnaissance which provided valuable intelligence for operations in the Central Pacific.

And it was during those operations that the true worth of Tarawa became apparent. The knowledge and experience gained there led to great improvements in amphibious landing techniques, and substantially reduced the cost of the landings that followed. For example, the value of accurate naval and air bombardment against selected targets was appreciated, when it became apparent that the defenders could not be blasted out of their well prepared defences by a brief general bombardment, however powerful. Mounting a longer and more precise bombardment, and timing its effect around the landing of the first troops ashore, became a major aim. Difficulties of supporting the troops ashore were noted and ironed out. The marines themselves analysed the effectiveness of their weapons, and their experience led to better teamwork, a more balanced selection of the weapons needed to reduce enemy strongholds, the development of flamethrowing light tanks, the provision of vastly increased numbers of amphibious landing vehicles for a Marine Division, and perhaps most important, the use of portable and waterproof-communications equipment, to keep the men ashore in close touch with the landing force commanders.

As the American drive across the Central Pacific progressed, the lessons learned on Tarawa were put to good use, and the enormous cost of the operation was to a great extent vindicated.

In paying that cost, the Marines established a reputation for personal energy and courage which shines throughout Henry Shaw's enthralling book. It is not an epic story. In a sense, it is military history on a small scale. No great armies of troops were engaged in month-long operations that spanned the breadth of continents. Tarawa itself is not even large enough to merit a mention in any but the most detailed western atlases. And only one Marine Division was involved, in a battle which raged furiously for three days, then was quiet.

But their impact was unparalleled. In that short space of time, they put the name of Tarawa indelibly on the world map; they confirmed the reputation of the Marines as a fighting force without superior; and they added a new name to the roll of great American battles. As Time Magazine said:

'Last week some two or three thousand US Marines, most of them now dead or wounded, gave the nation a name to stand beside those of Concord Bridge, the Bonhomme Richard, the Alamo, Little Big Horn, and Belleau Wood. The name was Tarawa.'

Why Tarawa?

Until November of 1943, the name Tarawa was buried deep in obscure pages of the history of Pacific exploration and colonial expansion. Except to certain planners in Washington and Tokyo, and the men responsible for executing their plans, this small atoll and its main island, Betio, were virtually unknown. Then, in a brief span of time, 'seventy six stark and bitter hours' that island was taken. And the man who commanded its captors could truthfully say that in the battle there the 'heroism of both attackers and defenders is worthy to stand beside the most renowned in the history of warfare'.

Tarawa lies some 2,500 miles southwest of Pearl Harbor and 1,300 miles Southeast of Truk, which was the main Japanese bastion in the Central Pacific during the early years of World War II. The strategic value of Tarawa in 1943 lay in its location. It was the most important atoll in the Gilbert Islands, headquarters of the Japanese garrison and site of the island group's only airfield. To the North and West were Japanese bases in the Marshalls and Carolines, to the South and East were Allied-held islands that guarded the lifeline from Hawaii and the US to the South Pacific, New Zealand, and Australia.

Most Allied operations in 1942 and the first six months of 1943 were aimed at securing that lifeline. The roll-back of Japanese forward positions in the South and Southwest Pacific started in August 1942 with seizure of Guadalcanal in the southern Solomons and the securing of Papua in eastern New Guinea. In 1943 the methodical advance continued, with each objective determined in large part by its suitability as an airbase, and its location within range of friendly land-based fighter aircraft.

By late summer, naval and land forces under Vice-Admiral William Halsey, Commander South Pacific, had reached New Georgia in the central Solomons and begun the construction of a series of fighter and bomber fields near Munda. His next target was to be Cape Torokina on Bougainville where another airfield complex would be built. To the West, General Douglas MacArthur's Southwest Pacific forces were moving into position to strike at

Cape Gloucester on the opposite end of the large island of New Britain from the Japanese headquarters at Rabaul. With Cape Gloucester in his hands, MacArthur could move safely through the Dampier Straits between New Guinea and New Britain and attack west along New Guinea's coast towards the Philippines.

This concept of operations grew out of the debates and arguments of representatives of Southwest, South, and Central Pacific leaders who met with members of the JCS staff in Washington in March 1943. At this Pacific Military Conference, MacArthur's plan of operations leading to the capture of Rabaul was presented, as were also his troop requirements: five additional infantry divisions and

five more air groups. Neither the men nor the planes were available and a less ambitious set of goals had to be agreed upon. In 1943, the general's forces and those of Admiral Halsey, who operated under his strategic direction, would occupy Woodlark and Kiriwina Islands, continue operations on New Guinea, seize footholds on New Georgia and Bougainville, and land on western New Britain.

The beneficiary of this reduced scale of MacArthur's operations was Admiral Chester Nimitz, Commander-in-Chief Pacific Fleet and Pacific Ocean Areas. He could now advance across the Central Pacific, which in the eyes of the Navy member of the JCS, Admiral Ernest J King, was the most direct and practical route to Japan

Three architects of the Pacific offensive: Nimitz, King, and Halsey

Dotted throughout the vast stretches of ocean were island objectives, potential air and naval bases, that could be isolated by carrier task forces and captured by amphibious troops. It was clear at least to Navy officers that the war in the Pacific was essentially a naval campaign and that America's tremendous and growing seapower should be exploited to the fullest to bring Japan to her knees.

The American and British Combined Chiefs-of-Staff, meeting in Washington in May 1943, accepted the new strategy. The British, however, made clear their objection to any step-up of operations in the Pacific which would adversely affect the drive against Germany. While the defeat of Germany was affirmed as the number one Allied objective, and the CCS was given a veto power over Pacific plans, the future looked bright for a greater American effort in the Pacific. In 1943 however, the means at hand were limited and several agreed objectives in Washington were later deferred for less ambitious targets. The decision to wrest control of the Gilberts from the Japanese was one such change of plan.

The initial objective in the Central Pacific drive was to have been the Marshall Islands, which had been in Japanese hands since the First World War. Little was known of these 'mystery islands', but the defenses were believed to be strong and the garrison large. In addition, the naval and air base at Truk, which posed a threat of both land and carrier-based air attacks, was far closer to the proposed objectives in the Marshalls than it was to the Gilberts. An attack on the Marshalls was a calculated risk that few men of higher authority or responsibility were prepared to take.

In the light of what happened later in the Pacific fighting – and not too much later – it is hard for the armchair strategist to see why Tarawa was a necessary target, but no amount of hindsight can match the pressures and realities of the existing situation. The American fleet was rebuilding but still it was not strong. The forces available for the two-pronged attack, MacArthur's and Nimitz's, were not impressive. The decision was made to seize a first objective in the Central Pacific that could be readily taken with the available resources – or so it seemed at the time.

By the middle of 1942 the Japanese had reached the limit of their expansion in the Pacific. They had fatally overextended themselves, although this was not apparent at the time. Their possessions formed a 'salient' in the Southern Pacific, and it was resolved to 'Pinch Off' this bulge with offensives in New Britain, the Solomons, and the Gilberts. The target selected in the Gilberts was Tarawa

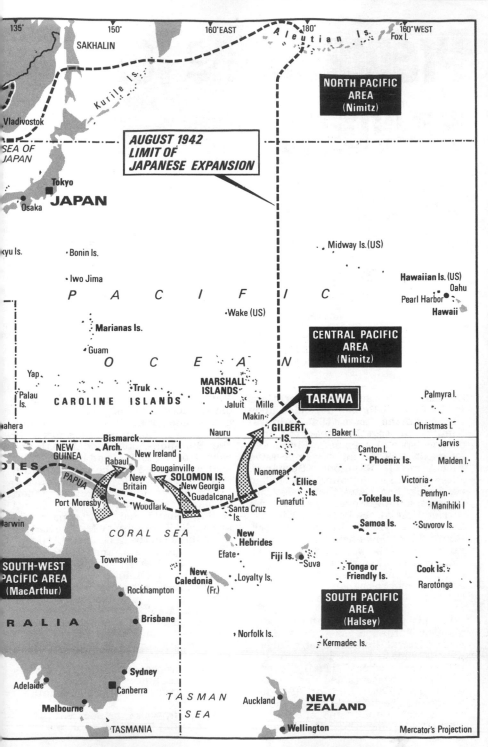

Preparations for Galvanic

So much of the success of operations in the Central Pacific depended upon the command team that Admiral Nimitz put together that the men deserve special mention. First, and foremost, was the quietly impressive Vice-Admiral Raymond Spruance. Although his background was that of the 'black shoe' Navy, the battleships, cruisers, and destroyers, he had led a carrier force at the Battle of Midway, and led it to victory in what was certainly the decisive naval battle of the early days of the war. Spruance was a planner, a thinker, a man who inspired respect in associates and subordinates; he had the capability of getting the best out of those who worked for him.

For his principal amphibious commander, Spruance asked for and got Rear-Admiral Richmond Kelly Turner. Kelly Turner was a driving, aggressive taskmaster, whose usually proper manner and bespectacled visage masked his grim determination. He could explode and he did on occasion, enough to warrant a nickname of 'Terrible Turner' to some who felt his wrath.

But he was, like Spruance, a vastly experienced naval officer and one who commanded respect if not affection. He had led the amphibious forces in the Solomons, at Guadalcanal and New Georgia, and he had the expertise that was needed for the new offensive. So did his ground force counterpart.

For his senior troop commander, Spruance wanted Major-General Holland Smith and Nimitz made him available. The doughty Marine had led amphibious corps in both the Atlantic and Pacific Fleets, and trained both Army and Marine divisions in the tactics and techniques of amphibious assault. He was the possessor of a nickname too, a play on his initials, 'Howling Mad'. Like Turner, Holland Smith did not suffer fools gladly; he demanded and got maximum effort from those who served under him. His anger was legendary, yet his outward appearance was deceptively benign. Behind his steel-rimmed glasses, however, his eyes were notably

Nimitz, *left*, walks the deck with Vice-Admiral Raymond Spruance.

Opposite: Lieutenant-General Holland M Smith, left, with Vice-Admiral Richmond Kelly Turner at Iwo Jima. Both were promoted after Tarawa. *Above:* Major-General Julian C Smith, 2nd Marine Division Commander

lacking in humor when there was a job to be done.

Kelly Turner and Holland Smith were a well-matched pair. Their arguments were forceful, their opinions strong. In many ways they balanced each other and, as Spruance had expected, they worked things out between themselves to get their work done. It is a pity – or perhaps to the more sensitive, a blessing – that their top-level planning sessions were not put on tape. Naval history would have been enlivened for generations to come!

But the point to be made about these men, to whom their country owes an enormous debt, was that they were professionals in the finest military sense of that word. They were teachers as well as inspiring leaders, and they set the pattern of amphibious warfare

17

in the climactic years of the battles in the Pacific. The staff officers they trained and the commanders they developed were the men who directed an unprecedented parade of victories that began at Tarawa and ended at Iwo Jima and Okinawa.

At the outset of the planning phase for the Gilberts, dubbed 'Operation Galvanic', Admiral Spruance established the command pattern that had held true at Guadalcanal. The amphibious troops commander, Smith, was to be completely subordinate to the amphibious force commander, Turner. This arrangement did not last very long in the face of the Marine's vigorous objections. Soon he and Turner faced each other as equals at the planning table, but once underway Spruance made it clear that Turner was to have the final say-so. And the objectives chosen were so small, relatively speaking, that there would be no need until the Marianas were hit for Holland Smith, as a corps commander, to exercise control ashore. That responsibility in the Gilberts went to two other generals named Smith. One, Major-General Julian Smith, led the veteran 2nd Marine Division; the other, Major-General Ralph Smith, commanded the untested 27th Infantry Division, formerly a New York National Guard outfit.

Julian Smith's Marines were scheduled to take Tarawa: a reinforced regiment of Ralph Smith's division was slated to seize Makin, another atoll in the Gilberts. Makin had not been one of the original objectives selected for 'Galvanic', but it was substituted for a much harder nut to crack, Nauru Island, some 380 miles west of Tarawa. Once they had had a look at their resources and assessed the Japanese threat from Truk and from the Marshalls to the north Spruance, Turner, and Holland Smith wanted no part of Nauru. The thought of conducting simultaneous amphibious operations separated by a day's hard sailing for fast ships, and with no possibility for land-based aerial search to scout possible enemy attacks, seemed to Spruance to be 'extremely unwise and hazardous'.

He recalled his deliberations with his senior commanders:

'Kelly Turner and I both discussed this situation with Holland Smith at length. It appeared to me that Nauru had been useful to the Japanese position from which to search to the southward the area between the Gilbert and Ellice Groups on the east and the Solomons on the west. Once this area was controlled by us, Nauru was not needed by us, and we could keep it pounded down. On the other hand, Makin was one hundred miles closer to the Marshalls where we were going, and it tied in well from the point of view of fleet coverage with an operation against Tarawa. The more we studied the details of capturing Nauru, the tougher the operation appeared to be, and finally it seemed doubtful that the troops assigned for it could take it. The transports assigned for trooplift were the limiting factor. Makin... was an entirely satisfactory objective, and its capture was well within our capabilities.'

In Holland Smith's appraisal of the situation, he pointed out that it would take a division to capture Nauru, which was believed to be heavily defended, and that the prize was not worth the effort. The island did not have good beaches or much of an airfield, and its small lagoon could not accommodate large ships. Instead, Makin, which appeared to have a much smaller garrison and a much bigger lagoon, was more favorably situated for control of the Gilberts. The proposed target substitution was presented to Admiral King when he was at Pearl Harbor on 24th September. The Navy's senior officer was convinced, as Nimitz had been, and promised to carry the recommendation back to the JCS. Once he was back in Washington, King had no apparent difficulty in persuading his colleagues to substitute Makin for Nauru.

One other objective, Apamama (Abemama) Atoll, remained in the Galvanic plan. Reasonably sure that the atoll was lightly defended, the American commanders vizualized no trouble in its capture and viewed it as an insurance dividend that would give them the site of an airfield and an anchorage that could help maintain control of the Gilberts. So, as the Galvanic plan finally evolved, it called for the simultaneous seizure of Tarawa, Makin, and Apamama, the first objective by an understrength division, the second by a reinforced regiment, and the third by a company. Tarawa was, as it had been since the inception of planning, the primary target.

The task of making the amphibious assault on Betio and of securing the rest of the atoll fell naturally to the 2nd Marine Division. No younger than the 1st Marine Division, since both had been activated on the same day (1st February 1941), the 2nd had also fought on Guadalcanal. One of its regiments, the 2nd Marines, had landed in the initial assault as a replacement for a 1st Division regiment garrisoning Samoa. Both of the 2nd Division's other infantry regiments, the 6th and 8th Marines, its artillery regiment, the 10th Marines, and its engineers, the 18th Marines, had come in as reinforcements and seen the campaign through to its end in February 1943. The division commander never reached the 'Canal', however, since Major-General John Marston was senior to the Army general who was in command of the final stages of the operation. Regardless of this sore point in inter-service etiquette, most of the units of the 2nd Division shared with the 1st its award of the Presidential Unit Citation for heroic service in the capture and defense of Guadalcanal. After Tarawa there would be another such award, this one clearly and unquestionably the 2nd's private decoration.

From the jungles of the Solomons, the now battle-tested troops of the 2nd Division sailed for New Zealand's North Island to rest and rehabilitation camps in and around Wellington. The change of climate and atmosphere was welcome; many of the men had contracted malaria and dengue fever; others were suffering from 'jungle rot', the name given to a dozen varieties of ubiquitous skin infections. Wellington with its friendly air, its marvellous beer, and its lively girls proved a welcome tonic. The Americans benefited greatly from the absence of many New Zealand men in the war zones of Asia, Europe, and Africa. Like the 1st Division, which had similar experiences in its camps near Melbourne, Australia, the 2nd's Marines found themselves to be both popular and unusually successful in

their love life. The mutual admiration society with the distaff New Zealanders had an inevitable result; hundreds of marriages were contracted. For the next two decades, New Zealand (and Australian) wives were far from unusual in any gathering of Marine families.

While New Zealand, and particularly Wellington, established themselves indelibly in the 2nd Division's history and lore, the purpose of the visit there was never forgotten. The division was to restore its health, absorb casualty replacements, and prepare for battle again. A progressive training program was initiated which laid emphasis first on small unit tactics and then moved on to manoeuvres of larger and larger elements. In the hills outside Wellington, on firing ranges, and in whatever amphibious craft could be borrowed, the division made ready for its next operation. No Marine is ever allowed to forget that he is a sea soldier, that the reason for his existence is amphibious assault, and the 2nd Division was no exception.

Nothing in warfare can be more confusing than a landing in the face of enemy fire. The need for intricate co-ordination of air and naval fire support, of landing craft and assault shipping, of troops and weapons, and of a host of other details occurs nowhere else in war. And the veterans – the real veterans, the senior officers and NCOs who had taken part in the landing exercises of the 1930's, when American amphibious doctrine was thrashed out and refined – knew that they and the younger men would face a trying ordeal no matter what their objective was.

There was an answer to this promise of confusion in the amphibious assault – small unit leadership. The watchword of the division was 'Keep Moving', and every corporal, sergeant, lieutenant, and captain was imbued with this spirit by his superiors. If an officer or NCO fell, there would be a man to step into his place.

In the summer of 1943, the average Marine in New Zealand had no idea where he was going to fight next, and to tell the truth, not many cared much. One fight is as good as another, if you have to fight. But a few men knew what was to happen, and a heavily-guarded war room was established in the Windsor Hotel in Wellington, as Divisional headquarters, where advance planning for Tarawa began. General Julian Smith and his senior staff members got their first word of the target from Admiral Spruance, who came to Wellington in early August. One look at the map of Betio and the reefs surrounding it was enough to convince the Marines that getting across those reefs would be their biggest problem in the landing. General Smith's operations officer, Lieutenant-Colonel David Shoup, asked for some of the plastic boats he had heard were being tested for shallow water use. None were available. As far as the Navy was concerned, the landing would have to be made in ships' boats.

This situation started a new train of thought, one that was to prove essential to the success of 'Galvanic'. Why not use amphibious tractors (LVTs) for the assault waves. They could not be stopped whether there was water over the reef or not. The LVTs had been employed previously as supply vehicles in a ship-to-shore role and proved so useful at this task that the 1st Division had strong reservations about their being put to any other use. Not so the 2nd Division; it had the reefs of Tarawa to face.

The model that had been used at Guadalcanal, the LVT(1) was unarmored and highly vulnerable to all types of enemy fire. The division's 2nd Amphibian Tractor Battalion had a hundred of these vehicles, many of them nearing the end of their useful running life. Mechanics were able to salvage seventy-five LVT-1s, but this was not enough to land the three assault waves that general Smith wanted to put ashore in 'amtracs'. The division pushed hard to get more tractors, enlisting the support of General Holland Smith's V Amphibious Corps (VAC) staff. The Corps, in turn, argued long and heatedly with the Navy, which had some strong reservations, not so much about the use of the tractors but rather about the means to get them to the target. There were some new armored models, LVT(2)s, available on the West Coast, but they could not get out to New Zealand in time to join the 2nd Division. They would have to marry up with their crews at some intermediate point and then proceed to the target in slow-moving tank landing ships (LSTs). The LST convoys would have to precede the main troops shipping to the target in order to arrive on schedule on D-Day. Admiral Turner was reluctant to chance the discovery of the LSTs by Japanese scout planes or submarines; he thought this premature disclosure of American intentions might jeopardize the surprise he wanted to achieve.

Despite the problems raised by the employment of the LVT(2)s, the Marines were adamant. They wanted them. And with Admiral Nimitz's support they got them. A provisional company from the 2nd Amtrac Battalion, ten officers and about 300 drivers, crewmen, and mechanics, left New Zealand for Samoa, where it met a shipment of fifty of the new tractors, which had been sent out from San Diego in the LSTs that were to carry them to the Gilberts.

Although the newer model looked much like its predecessor, it had a more powerful radial engine with 200 horsepower instead of 146, and it could carry twenty fully-equipped assault troops, two more than the LVT(1), and carry them a little faster, making about four knots. And most important, the LVT(2) was armored, not heavily, but enough to give some protection on front, sides, and cab against small arms fire and shell fragments. Back in New Zealand, an attempt was made to bring the LVT(1)s closer to this standard by attaching boiler plate specially made by the local Ford Motor Company plant to the windows of the cabs, giving at least some cover to the drivers.

While the essential business of equipping the assault waves was going on, a process that spanned most of the preparatory phase of the operation, the other elements of the complex amphibious planning process were going forward at all naval and landing force staff levels. Admiral Turner, in view of the short time given him to prepare for Galvanic, relied a great deal on high level conferences at Pearl Harbor to thrash out problems that arose. The face-to-face confrontation of the senior commanders, the men who could make the final decisions, vastly speeded preparations – although the arguments could and did get heated at times. There were hordes of problems to be met, not the least of which was the separation of the 2nd Marine Division from the rest of the assault force.

Julian Smith and members of his staff flew to Pearl on 2nd October, to present the 2nd Division's scheme of maneuver and to present a strong case for a preliminary landing on an island adjacent to Betio. The division commander was a courtly gentleman whose 'entirely unassuming manner and friendly hazel eyes clothed a determined personality that could be forcefully displayed in decisive moments'. This was one of those moments. He wanted artillery landed on an offshore island in order to improve the chances of his Marines in the assault. Holland Smith had to tell him that it could not be done. The Japanese were believed to be capable of launching a combined air and submarine attack within three days after the assault force arrived in the Gilberts. No time could be devoted to secondary landings; if this happened, the vulnerable and scarce transports and cargo vessels might be caught lying offshore and still partially loaded.

This disappointment did not really fill Julian Smith's cup of gall; the other bad news he received at Pearl filled it to overflowing. One of the division's infantry regiments would be held in corps reserve to be used either at Makin or Tarawa as the situation required. Not only would the Betio assault be made without preliminary artillery support, but it would be made by only two regimental combat teams. If the preliminary intelligence reports were right, and they were, the 4,000-plus Japanese at Tarawa, well dug-in in prepared defenses, would face only two times their number in assault troops, a decidedly poor ratio of attackers to defenders that boded ill for the Marines.

Having presented his arguments and lost them, except where the LVT(2)s were concerned, Julian Smith had his basic scheme of maneuver approved.

At his request, the VAC operation plan was worded so that the 2nd Marine Division was directed to seize control of Betio first before taking any of the other islands of Tarawa. He had to live with this decision by higher authority, but he did not ever want it thought that it was his decision.

While the 2nd Division staff group was at Pearl Harbor, it was able to co-ordinate its plans with the staff of the attack force that would transport, support, and land the Marines at Tarawa. Admiral Turner had chosen to lead the northern attack force at Makin, wearing two hats as both assault and attack force commander, in order to be at the point of greatest threat if the Japanese attacked from the Marshalls or Truk. To head the southern attack force, Rear-Admiral Harry Hill was chosen. A veteran battleship and escort carrier group commander from the South Pacific, Hill reported to Admiral Turner on 18th September. A confident and impressive officer, Hill had just a month to assemble a staff, join in the planning conferences, and get oriented to his task. On 19th October, only a few days after Julian's Smith's return to Wellington, Admiral Hill followed.

When he arrived in New Zealand, the admiral was less than happy to see what he had for amphibious shipping. His transport group commander, Captain Herbert Knowles, described the legion of problems he faced:

'Most of these ships arrived lacking full boat complements and woefully lacking in communication facilities. Some of the ships had been diverted to Wellington while still on "shakedown" operations . . . My flagship *Monrovia* had been stripped of everything useful in the way of communication facilities except basic commercial ship radios . . . . Had we not had extra naval personnel and Army SCRs (both "appropriated" at the end of the Aleutian Operation) we would have been in an even sorrier mess than we were. The few ships that had been in the Aleutians furnished officers and men to give at least a minimum of experienced personnel to the new arrivals.'

Admiral Hill faced a different aspect of the same make-shift/make-do situation. When he arrived in Wellington,

The LVT (Landing Vehicle Tracked) I. An amphibious vehicle, capable of surmounting reefs even at low tide, the LVT I proved invaluable at Betio. *Weight:* 27,500 pounds. *Length:* 23 feet. *Width:* 9 feet 10 inches. *Engine:* 146 brake horse power 6 cylinder Hercules. *Speed:* 12 mph (land), 7 knots (water). *Range:* 225 miles (land), 210 miles (water). *Crew:* 3. *Payload:* 4,500 pounds. *Armament:* Various, portable machine guns

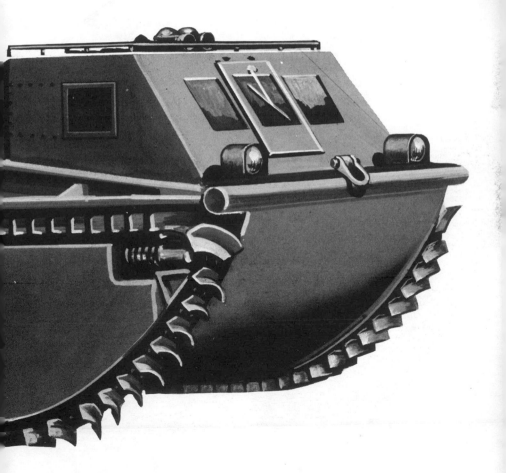

The LVT (Landing Vehicle Tracked) II. This faster, stronger version of the LVT I, had better armament and a lower silhouette. *Weight:* 27,600 pounds. *Length:* 25 feet 11 inches. *Width:* 10 feet 9 inches. *Engine:* 250 horse power Continental. *Payload:* 4,500 pounds. *Crew:* 4. *Speed:* 20 mph (land), 7½ knots (water). *Range:* 200 miles (land), 60 miles (water). *Armament.* One .30 Browning, and one .5 Browning

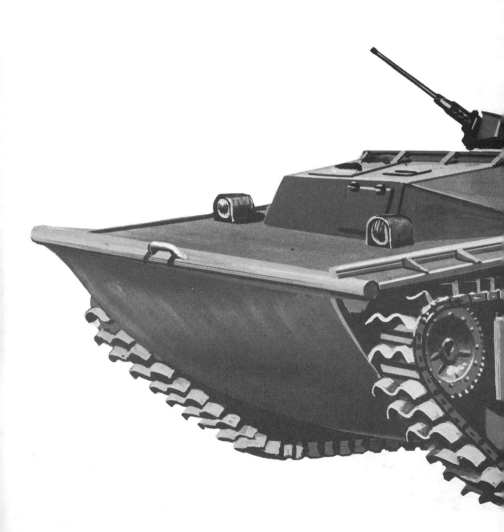

some twenty yard workmen were still on board his flag, the battleship *Maryland*, making necessary alterations for its role at Tarawa. The only place where the essential communication center could be built in the time allotted was on the wing of the flag bridge, and the bridge was at about on the same level as the muzzles of the main battery 16-inch guns when they were raised to fire at medium ranges. The potential for trouble in this arrangement was fully realized at Tarawa. Although the need for specially-equipped amphibious command ships had been recognized and they were being rushed to completion, none would be available for Galvanic.

Despite the problems, the preparations for the coming operation accelerated. As Knowles' transports arrived from all over the Pacific, they were put to work landing 2nd Division Marines in training exercises. Landing craft (LCVPs and LCMs), and crews from the boat pool at Wellington found themselves filling out ships' complements and transporting Marines and their tanks, trucks, and guns in mock assault waves against practise beaches. Although the actual target of the division was a closely-held secret, the scheme of maneuver and the men who would make the initial landings were now well known. The division operation order was completed on 25th October.

Basically, the responsibility for securing a beach-head on Betio would rest on Combat Team 2, the 2nd Marines reinforced by the 2nd Battalion, 8th Marines. Combat Team 8 (less 2/8) would constitute the division reserve. The onerous task of serving as VAC reserve fell to Combat Team 6, and its men were not too happy about the prospect of missing the main event – whatever it might be. The razzing they would take if they didn't get into the coming scrap was not hard to imagine. Each of the combat teams had elements of all the division's units, artillery, tanks, engineers, and service troops, attached to it for the landing, with the preponderance of strength going to Combat Team 2.

As the time to mount out drew near, speculation was rife among the junior officers and enlisted men about

the next operation. Rumors reached epidemic proportions and touched on a dozen targets, among them Tarawa. But the high level secrecy was real, and neither the target nor the time of its attack was widely known. Elaborate cover plans were formulated to keep the destination and time of departure a secret. Ostensively as the end of October neared, the next move of the division was to be a full-scale practise landing at Hawkes Bay near Wellington followed by a return to the city. Seabags were packed and green dress uniforms were carefully folded away for hopeful use on liberty when the ships returned. Arrangements were made with the Royal New Zealand Air Force to fly supporting strikes for the landing exercise and with the railway to transport heavy equipment back to Wellington from the landing beaches.

Finally, when everyone and everything was loaded for the exercise, General Smith and Colonel Shoup 'drove to see the Governor General and told him'. Shoup recalled that 'he was the only one in New Zealand who actually knew we were headed for battle and not coming back. Hotels were full of Marine clothing, cars were parked in the streets, dates were coming up for the weekend.'

The actual destination of the convoy was Efate in the New Hebrides, where Captain Knowles' transports would join the rest of Admiral Hill's attack force and conduct rehearsals for the landing. Three days out, the ships' address systems announced that the Marines of the 3rd Division had landed on Bougainville in the northern Solomons. The news was greeted with resounding shouts by the men on the decks and in the holds. The sentiment was genuine; many men had friends in the ranks of the 3rd, but even those who didn't cheered. The Marine Corps then, as now, had all the *esprit de corps* of the small outfit it had been before World War II, and there was, and is, a real feeling of brotherhood among Marines. This general spirit, coupled with natural unit pride, was to stand the 2nd Division in good stead in its ordeal to come.

It would be 14th November before Admiral Hill authorized the dis-

Landing craft and tanks are loaded aboard the transport ships at
Wellington, New Zealand

closure of target details to the men on board ship, but when the word came it was chilling – and as events would prove surprisingly accurate. The intelligence collection and evaluation effort for Galvanic was outstanding.

When the target was selected very little was known of the Gilberts, despite their long possession by the British. The hydrographic charts and tide tables available proved to be little better, and in some cases no better, than those produced by the Wilkes expedition which visited the Central Pacific islands in 1841. Much more accurate information about the atolls, their reefs, passages, and lagoons, and about the tidal ranges was needed. It was to come from three sources, aerial photographs, submarine reconnaissance, and former residents of the Gilberts.

On 17th/18th September, aircraft from three of the Pacific Fleet's large carriers struck Makin, Tarawa, Apamama, and Nauru, blasting the enemy and photographing his defenses. The Navy pilots were joined in both phases of these attacks by B-24s of the 7th Air Force, operating from forward airfields on Canton and Funafuti Islands. The Liberators returned on the 19th, again mixing bombs with photography. The pictures taken then, and in another combined mission a month later on 20th October, formed the basis for much of the intelligence gleaned about Tarawa. The aerial camera had its limitations, however, and the combination of vertical and oblique shots answered only some of the many questions that plagued the planners.

Much more was learned during a daring cruise of the submarine *Nautilus*, which spent nearly three weeks in September cruising through the Gilberts. The submarine logged information on the prevailing tides and currents at each of the atoll objectives. With a special rig on its periscope that held one of its officer's cameras (none of the issued cameras worked properly) and permitted sequence timing for stereo overlap, the *Nautilus* took a series of pictures that provided clear, panoramic views of the targets. These photos, and the vital hydrographic information, reached Pearl Harbor on 7th October.

To supplement the intelligence gathered by the planes and submarine, Admiral Turner had his 'Foreign Legion'. This was a group of sixteen men familiar with the islands, all of whom had traded, travelled, or resided in the Gilberts before the coming of the Japanese forced them to flee south to more friendly waters. While all the islanders shared their knowledge with Turner's amphibious planners, those who knew Tarawa best were sent to Wellington to work with the 2nd Marine Division staff. The most ticklish question they were called upon to answer was how much water would flow over the reef on the morning of 20th November 1943, the day chosen for the assault.

The opinions varied, the existing tide tables varied; there was no sure way of resolving the argument. Some of the men were sure that on the 20th, during the third quarter of the moon, there would be as much as five feet of a neap tide covering the reef. Neap tides have the least ebb and flow and produce the lowest high tides. Other islanders, principally Major FLG Holland, a New Zealander who had lived at Tarawa, were less certain of this judgment, although the islander-produced tide tables appeared to prove it. Holland pointed out that during neap periods at Tarawa, the tides had often ebbed and flowed irregularly and perhaps as little as three feet of water would cover the reef.

The crucial interest of the Marines in the water depth centered on the possibility that landing craft would not make it over the reef. The majority of the assault and supporting troops of the division had to land by ships' boats followed the initial waves of LVTs, and most of the follow-on flow of weapons, vehicles, ammunition, water, and rations would come in by boat also. An LCVP fully loaded drew three and a half feet and if it grounded at the reef's edge or on the way in, its passengers would have to wade to shore, carrying, pushing, or dragging their weapons and equipment with them. As the 2nd Division Chief-of-Staff, Colonel Marritt Edson, was to note:

'. . . we had a pretty slim margin anyhow; even if we had three and one-half

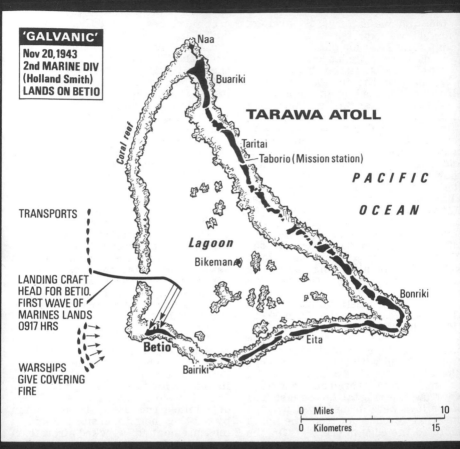

'GALVANIC'

Nov 20, 1943
2nd MARINE DIV
(Holland Smith)
LANDS ON BETIO

Naa

Buariki

TARAWA ATOLL

Coral reef

Taritai

Taborio (Mission station)

P A C I F I C

O C E A N

TRANSPORTS

LANDING CRAFT
HEAD FOR BETIO.
FIRST WAVE OF
MARINES LANDS
0917 HRS

Lagoon

Bikeman

Bonriki

WARSHIPS
GIVE COVERING
FIRE

Betio

Eita

Bairiki

| 0 | Miles | 10 |
| 0 | Kilometres | 15 |

The Tarawa Atoll showing the position of Betio, the Marines prime target,
and the positions of the transports and the covering warships for the assault

to four and one-half feet, the average four feet we expected, that gave us damn little edge for our LCVPs and gave us practically no edge for the LCMs that had tanks on them.'

Faced with the terrible responsibility of commanding an amphibious assault landing against a determined enemy, General Julian Smith had no intention of deluding the men who were to hit Betio's beaches. At all briefings, the Marines of the fourth and following waves were told that they might have to wade ashore, that the tides might not float their boats. The armor commanders made preparations to have guides wade ahead of the lumbering, half-blind tanks to lead them to the beaches, and the artillery officers reminded the crews of the 75mm pack howitzers that they could well end up manhandling the pieces and their ammunition through the water.

The reefs themselves were formidable obstacles, stretching from 600 to 1100 yards out from Betio's shores. The island itself was little wider at any point that the narrowest part of the reef shelf and with a form somewhat like a bird, stretched about two and a half miles from its head on the west to a narrow, tapering tail on the east. The bird's legs were formed by a wooden pier that reached out from the north shore to the edge of the reef. On the south or ocean shore, the barrier reef, which lay well away from the island, was coursed by heavy swells. The waters off the western headland, swept by strong and irregular currents, contained both barrier and fringing reef formations. The choice of landing beaches, therefore, had narrowed to the northern shore, helped on by the realization that the island itself would shield ships in the lagoon from foul weather and the fact that aerial photos showed the enemy defenses concentrated their greatest strength on the ocean side. Extensive minefields were evident on the southern and western beaches, but few mines were noted on the lagoon side which the Japanese were using as the entry for fortification material and supplies. It was evident that the enemy intended to seal the shores of Betio against all comers, but the work was still going on when the photo-

graphic planes snapped their record.

The layout of Tarawa encouraged the Americans to make their landing from the lagoon. Triangular-shaped, the atoll was twenty-two miles long with a twelve and a half mile base at its southern end where Betio was its westernmost island. The only passage into the lagoon, a mile-wide break in the western barrier reef, lay three and a half miles north-west of the northern corner of Betio. There was little evidence of enemy defenses or activity anywhere else at Tarawa except at Betio, and it appeared there was little risk from Japanese guns on any of the numerous tiny islets and narrow islands that nestled in the reef on the southern and eastern sides of the lagoon. Planners could figure, then, on moving into the lagoon with the assault waves and some escorts and concentrating their attention on Betio. But if there were no guns on the other islands, there was no lack of them on the target island.

Photo interpreters, scanning every millimeter of the prints they received of Betio, came up with a formidable gun count. They found there were at least eight large coast defense guns, including four 8 in. naval rifles. The 2nd Division intelligence officers determined the size of these cannon by relating their dimensions to known measurements of wrecked aircraft on Betio's airfield. In addition to the big pieces, the photos revealed twenty-five heavy and medium anti-aircraft guns and emplacements for eighty-two anti-boat guns and fifty-two machine guns. An actual after-battle count of major Japanese weapons noted twenty large cannon, ranging in size from 80mm to 8 inches, twenty-five field pieces (37mm, 70mm, and 75mm), seven light tanks with 37mm guns, and thirty-one 13mm machine guns. No accurate tally could be made of the number of light 7.7mm machine guns that the defenders had manned, for most them lay blasted or buried in the ruins of enemy emplacements. One notable, and thankful, absense from this arsenal was mortars; if the Japanese had any significant number on Betio they went undetected.

A stroke of genius, or perhaps just plain luck, enabled the intelligence officers to come within a few men of estimating the size of Tarawa's garrison. On a remarkable clear photograph of Betio, one that Lieutenant Colonel Shoup called 'the best single aerial photo taken during the Second World War', the interpreters spotted the shoreline latrines used by the Japanese. The detail was sharp enough so that some better-constructed types could be identified, ones that presumably were reserved for officer use. Estimating how many men the Japanese would assign to each latrine, the Americans came up with a garrison strength very close to the actual figure of 4,836 men. From order of battle intelligence the division received from VAC, its officers were reasonably sure that most, if not all, of the enemy forces were naval troops and that some of them were laborers and of dubious combat value.

There was little question, however, about the combat efficiency of the enemy naval infantry and gunners. Often dubbed by combat correspondents as Japanese Marines, the men of the Special Naval Landing Forces (SNLF) had proved themselves in earlier battles to be versatile, well-trained, and tenacious fighters. The SNLF units were usually equipped for the jobs they were given, and in defensive situations had been known to be heavily armed with crew-served weapons in impressive numbers.

The man who was charged with the defense of the Gilberts was Rear Admiral Keiji Shibasaki, commanding the 3rd Special Base Force with headquarters at Betio. This unit which had 1,122 men at Tarawa, had been known as 6th Yokosuka SNLF, incorporating the name of its home naval base in its title. Also at Tarawa, Shibasaki had the 7th Sasebo SNLF with 1,497 men, the 111th Construction Unit with 1,247 laborers, and 970 men of a Fourth Fleet Construction Department Detachment. The labor troops, the majority of whom were Koreans, were not combat trained and the Koreans, at least, were not at all eager for battle. The Makin Atoll garrison was a small model of that at Tarawa with 284 SNLF troops, about one hundred aviation personnel, and 446 laborers. On Apamama there were twenty-three Japanese.

While Admiral Shibasaki could only count about 3,000 of his men at Tarawa as combat effective, he got his full value from the remainder. The laborers contributed as much as the SNLF to the defense of Betio. The Army's official history of the Gilberts and Marshalls campaigns called Tarawa 'the most heavily defended atoll that would ever be invaded by Allied forces in the Pacific'. This appraisal added the opinion that with the possible exception of the beaches at Iwo Jima, Betio's 'were better protected against a landing force than any encountered in any theater of war throughout the Second World War'. There was good reason for this belief.

Betio was a veritable fortress. All along the island's shores were a series of strongpoints, pillboxes, and gun emplacements with carefully integrated fields of fire that permitted no 'blind side' approaches. The majority were completely covered and many had an inner core of reinforced concrete. Most were walled with alternating thick layers of resilient coconut logs and coral sand. These absorbent and protective layers were so effective that they defied direct hits by bombs and heavy shells. There was no way to knock out these defenses except by killing those who manned them.

In addition to the major weapons positions, there were scores of supporting rifle pits, trenches, and machine gun nests, also protected, with their fires interlocking to sweep the beaches and the waters beyond. Ringing the island about fifty to a hundred yards offshore was a double-apron barbed wire fence: concrete tetrahedrons studded the reefs, and barbed wire obstacles were placed in strategic locations along the beaches to channel assault troops into the fire lanes of weapons emplacements. A log barricade backed the beach on the south shore, converting it into a 20-foot wide death trap which could be blanketed by enemy small arms fire.

The beaches were the focal points of the Japanese defensive plan: the naval troops were told to 'knock out the landing boats with mountain gunfire, tank guns, and infantry guns, then concentrate all fires on the enemy's landing point and destroy him at the water's edge.' So prevalent was this all-out philosophy of stopping a landing at the beaches, there was no cohesive defense system inland. Aircraft revetments offered some cover to the defenders and there were scattered air raid shelters and trenches that had defensive potential. Huge reinforced concrete bunkers, many of them so covered by sand they resembled small hills, were scattered about the runways and taxi strips of the airfield. These goliaths housed the Japanese command posts, communications centers, and ammunition dumps and proved to be impervious to naval gunfire and bombs. No matter how formidable they appeared, however, they were built primarily for protection and not fighting. Once the guardian belt of coastal defenses was breached, these bunkers were vulnerable and could be sealed even though it was almost impossible for combat engineers to destroy them.

The reason for Betio's elaborate fortifications and strong garrison was not an isolated gesture of defiance. The enemy strategists figured that the Americans would attempt an advance across the Central Pacific and that the objectives would be the islands with airfields. If these islands were strongly held, the American amphibious vessels and supporting warships would be tied to their objectives long enough for Japanese aircraft and submarines to converge on them and attack. Then the enemy fleet would sortie from Truk and destroy the invaders. The Gilberts were to be part of an outer barrier of island defenses, stretching from the Marshalls to the Bismarcks, made secure by a combination of hard fighting garrisons and air and sea counter attacks. This was the essence of the Japanese plan but the Americans struck too soon and too powerfully for it to have much chance of success.

Admiral Shibasaki was sure of his own part in this overall scheme of defense. No matter what else miscued, Tarawa would be held. According to a prisoner taken on the island, the admiral said that the Americans couldn't take Betio with a million men in a hundred years.

About fifty-five per cent of the men of the 2nd Marine Division were combat veterans, but few of them had

participated in an opposed amphibious landing. All the men of the division, like all Marines, had a basic familiarity with amphibious techniques, landing craft, shipboard life as it was lived transport fashion, and most had had a chance to make a few practise landings in New Zealand. The intent of the stop at Efate was to rehearse the whole landing operation planned for Tarawa, to work out the inevitable kinks in the landing plans, and to familiarize the tractor and boat crews, the troops, and ships' companies with the disembarkation, boat-to-tractor transfer, and landing wave formation procedures.

The assault troops were landed at Mele Bay while the fire support ships simulated their bombardment at Pango Point. The fast carriers which would provide the D-Day aerial support were busy elsewhere in preparatory strikes and their planes did not take their role in the practise. A second full-scale rehearsal, following a critique of the flaws in the first, took place with the troops again landing at Mele and the warships actually firing a shore bombardment on Erradaku Island.

It was at this time, the pause at Efate, that the designated assault combat team commander, Colonel William Marshall, became ill. Unable to take a chance on Marshall's health on D-Day, General Julian Smith had to name a replacement. He choose the man most familiar with the division's plans, his operations officer, who was then spot promoted. Colonel Shoup, after taking command of the 2nd Marines, brought in his own executive officer, Lieutenant-Colonel Dixon Goen. Since he had worked in the same building and shared the same mess at Camp Paekakariki with the 2nd Marines' officers, Shoup was no stranger to them. The new regimental commander, a thick-set, bull-necked man with a hard-nosed attitude and a taste for poker and profanity, was to prove himself the right leader for the fight to come.

While Admiral Hill's Southern Attack Force (Task Force 52) rehearsed in the New Hebrides, a series of preliminary operations were underway designed to isolate and devastate the target islands. New forward bases at

Nanomea and Nukufetau Atolls in the Ellice Islands and at Baker Island to the east of the Gilberts had been occupied in August and September, and airfields were in operation at all three locations by 9th October. Liberators of the Seventh Air Force had been hitting the Gilberts and southern Marshalls all through the summer and early fall, but in a sporadic fashion. On 13th November, they began a systematic attack pattern with the Japanese airfields as their principal targets. Navy land-based bombers and seaplanes carried on night strikes on the Gilberts to keep up the pressure. Japanese aircraft fell prey to planes operating from the big carriers of Rear Admiral Charles A Pownall's Task Force 50 which struck Nauru on 18th November and hit Jaluit and Mille in the Marshalls on the 19th.

These attacks appeared to be successful in isolating the target area, but the real victory had been scored a couple of weeks earlier in the Southwest Pacific, in the air over Rabaul on New Britain. When Bougainville was assaulted, the Japanese carriers at Truk were emptied to send planes and pilots south to hit the American

General Julian C Smith and Admiral Hill

assault force. In a wild series of aerial battles, Army Air Forces and Navy fighters virtually destroyed the Japanese carrier complements. When Galvanic was launched, the enemy plan to attack the amphibious force and its covering ships when they struck the Gilberts was useless. Without their planes and pilots, the Japanese carriers were merely large sitting ducks. They could not be risked against Pownall's force. And without carrier cover, the enemy battleships and cruisers were equally helpless. So, although Admiral Spruance had no way of knowing it at the time, the Japanese fleet had no effective means of challenging the Galvanic expeditionary force. There would be submarine and air attacks, and there would be losses, but they would have no practical effect on the course of the operation.

On 13th November, Task Force 52 sortied from Efate, following its slower moving LST group which was carrying the LVT(2)s to Tarawa. At sea, on the 17th, Admiral Hill's ships rendezvoused with those of Admiral Turner which had come out from Hawaii, and the two attack forces followed a parallel course for the Gilberts. As the Navy had feared, the LSTs in advance of the main convoys

(in this case those with the LVT(2)s for the Makin landing) were spotted by a Japanese search plane on the 18th. Several enemy bombers appeared at dusk, but carrier planes shot down one and the rest disappeared. On the following day, a big patrol bomber was detected and destroyed. But there were no waves of enemy planes roaring in to attack the American ships. If the Japanese knew that an assault was coming, there appeared to be little that they could do about it until the island garrisons played their part.

On board the transports heading in for the target, the Marines now knew where they were going. Sealed packets of maps, photos and orders were broken out on all ships and small groups of men, intense and attentive in the sweltering equatorial heat, listened to briefings from their officers on what was coming. The men were told of the plans for preliminary bombardment by air, of the fact that cruisers from the fast carrier force would slam 8 in. rounds into Betio on D-minus 1 for two hours, to knock out the enemy's big guns. They listened to the scheme of preliminary air and naval gunfire bombardment, and it all looked and sounded good. Optimism seized some of the enlisted men and junior officers; Betio looked so small, and the weight of metal and explosives that would hammer it before the Marines ever landed was impressive. But most Marines were sceptical; they had fought the Japanese before and knew that they would battle to the death no matter what the odds were. And the odds were not as heavily weighted in favor of the attackers as they should have been.

On the decks of the convoy's ships, bayonets and knives were honed to razor sharpness, equipment was checked and re-checked, and when small arms ammunition was issued, the wise men looked over each round, clip, magazine, and belt. Rifles were cleaned and given a light coating of oil and then cleaned again and oiled again. There was an air of understandable nervousness overall, despite the quiet groups of half-naked card players, the solitary paperback readers, and the hundreds who just slept on the decks or stared out to sea and appeared to ignore what lay ahead.

Prelude to the Tarawa landings. Mass is said aboard a troop transport

Religious services were well attended and the congregations were serious.

Characteristically, Admiral Spruance, who accompanied the assault force in his flagship the cruiser *Indianapolis*, left the last-minute speeches to his subordinates. These exhortations were expected, well meant, and appreciated.

Admiral Turner's message to the attack force, read on D-minus 1 to

all hands, reminded the sailors and Marines of the 'close cooperation between all arms and services, the spirit of loyalty to each other, and the determination to succeed displayed by veteran and untried personnel alike,' which gave him complete confidence that 'we will never stop until we have achieved success.' In a similar vein, General Smith told his men that the division had been 'especially chosen by the high command for the assault on Tarawa because of its battle experience and com-bat efficiency.' He prophetically stated that what they did there would 'set a standard for all future operations in the Central Pacific area.' And he closed his message with two sentences that obviously touched the quietly listening men throughout the convoy: 'Your success will add new laurels to the glorious tradition of our Corps. Good luck and God bless you all.'

Assault
landing

During the early morning hours of D-Day, the scheme of attack called for the transports to move into an area off the lagoon entrance, about six miles from the chosen beaches. The LVT(1)s, carried on ten ships, would then be set in the water and move to the sides of three transports carrying men of Combat Team 2. As soon as the Marines of the first wave clambered down the heavy debarkation nets and into their appointed tractors, the second and third waves would follow and load into LCVPs. These boats would then rendezvous with the LVT-(2)s, which by then would have been disgorged by the LSTs. As the tractors moved to the wave assembly area

Dawn on D-Day. The landing craft of the assault waves assemble

north west of the lagoon passage, the Marines of the fourth and following waves would climb into their boats and help load heavy equipment and weapons. The LSD *Ashland*, which carried a company of medium tanks, would flood its well deck to enable its LCM-borne cargo to pass out its stern gate and join the massing assault. While the waves were forming, minesweepers would clear the reef passage, mark a channel, and then take up a position on the line of departure, where the long files of tractors and boats would make their right flank turn for the beaches.

While all this was going on, and just as dawn was breaking, planes from the big carriers were to open the attack on Betio with a half hour of strafing and bombing runs. As soon

as the aircraft pulled away, the fire support ships, three battleships, five cruisers, and nine destroyers, would open a two-hour bombardment. The first seventy-five minutes were to be devoted to neutralizing enemy defenses and knocking out coast defense guns, and the final forty-five minutes to increasingly heavy destructive fire which would saturate predetermined targets areas with high explosive. Then, as the assault waves were nearing the beaches, the carrier planes would return for a final five-minute strike on beach defenses.

Most of the fire support ships would be positioned in the open sea to the west of Betio firing down the long axis of the island, since shells coming from the south might well ricochet into the boat lanes. Two destroyers,

however, were to follow the minesweepers into the lagoon and take up positions where they could directly support the landing waves. Altogether, the formidable preliminary bombardment that had been planned was greater than any that had taken place yet in the Pacific. Some naval officers were convinced that there would be nothing worth noting left on the little island when the Marines landed. But Captain Knowles, who was one of the most experienced amphibious commanders in the attack force, felt differently and had said so forcibly in planning conferences. He recalled that in the Solomons, where

Overleaf: **The offshore support vessels lend weight to the attack with a heavy bombardment**

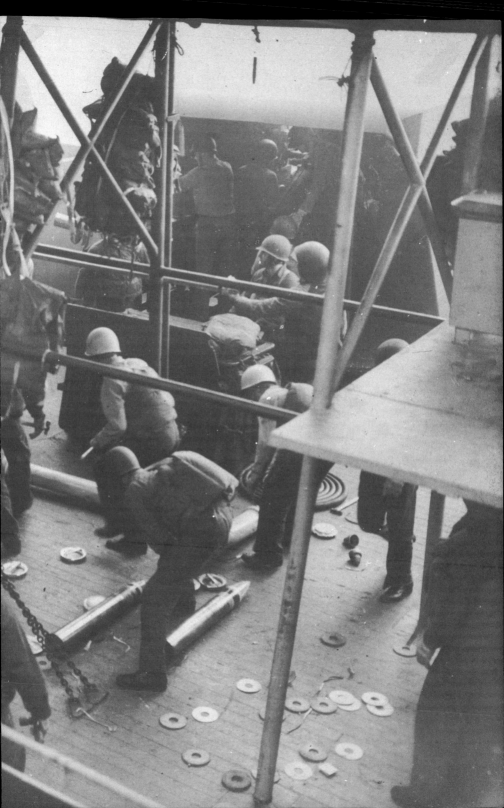

he had landed the 1st Parachute Battalion in its attack on Gavutu, 'from daylight to noon this little island was subjected to repeated bombing attacks and bombardment by cruisers and destroyers.' He pointed out that 'the results had been most disappointing.' And he feared they would be again.

On 20th November the moon rose shortly before one and the covering warships glided into position a little over one hour later. The low-lying atoll was silhouetted against the horizon as the transports hove to at about 0355 hours and immediately began unloading Marines of Combat Team 2. Admiral Hill soon discovered that these ships, beset by a 2 knot current, were drifting south into an area where they masked the fire of some of his gunfire support group. At 0431 hours the admiral ordered the transports to stop unloading and to move back to their proper positions. As the big ships shifted during the next half hour some of their trailing landing craft got lost and had to be rounded up, thus delaying the transfer of troops to tractors and the subsequent formation of the assault waves.

About ten minutes after Admiral Hill passed the word to the transports to move north, a red star cluster shot up through the darkness and burst over the eastern end of Betio. For a few moments nothing happened, and then at 0507 hours Japanese shore batteries opened fire. The splashes from misses were prodigious, indicating that the enemy still had his big coast defense guns which the bombers and cruisers had tried to knock out. Led by the 16 in. guns of the *Maryland*, the heavy support ships began firing in reply, seeking out the flashes of the enemy weapons. After *Maryland's* fifth salvo, a rewarding explosion ashore appeared to signal the end of Japanese 8 in. fire and the island lay quiet for a time as the pounding by battleships and cruisers continued. A pall of smoke and dust obscured the target, broken occasionally by pillars of fire when ammunition or fuel supplies were hit. In part to let this murky veil settle and to clear the way for a scheduled strike by carrier aircraft, the attack force commander signalled 'Cease firing'

at 0542 hours.

The Japanese took advantage of this pause in the rain of high explosive to open fire again, this time seeking out the transports which now could be distinguished in the gathering dawn. The near misses got too close for comfort; three sailors were hit by shell fragments. As soon as they had transferred the fourth wave into its boats, the transports sailed north out of range. With pardonable exaggeration the transport group commander noted in his report that for a half hour, 'the enemy was free to conduct target practise on the transports without interference by air or ship bombardment.'

It was not quite that long, but it must have seemed so. The planes were late. On board the *Maryland*, Admiral Hill's radio operators on the flag bridge were finding out that the concussion from the firing of the ship's main batteries had damaged some of their equipment. The admiral could not contact the planes and had no idea what had gone wrong. Apparently, a change of plan had been decided on to let the pilots attack after daybreak so that they could locate targets, but the word only reached the carrier group and, inexplicably, not the task force commander. At 0605, Hill ordered the ships' bombardment to continue, but the fire was soon lifted as the planes appeared a few minutes later. Now, however, in order to stay on schedule, the original thirty-minute air attack was cut to ten minutes.

As the aircraft struck Betio, it was still dark enough for the glare of tracers to blind the strafing fighter pilots in their Hellcats, but the dive bomber pilots seemed to have no trouble. To the thousands of eyes watching from the ships offshore and the tractors and boats bobbing in the choppy water, the air show was spectacular. Billows of dust rose high in the air mixed with plumes of flame as the planes worked their way' back and forth across Betio. When the strike groups drew away, the island was again obscured in a fire-flickered shroud. At least one senior pilot was

Above: Naval gun in action
Right: The LVTs splash towards Betio

skeptical about the results of the attack and he remarked that 'the great majority of all bombs merely dug a nice well and raised a great cloud of coral dust which hampered the bombing of other planes.'

After the carrier aircraft pulled out of the trajectory path of the naval guns, the shelling, this time the pre-landing bombardment, began again. The gunfire ships raked the island from one end to the other and poured shells into predetermined target areas often firing with the help of radar, as little could be seen through the thick haze. Almost as soon as the ships' batteries started lashing the island, the first three waves of tractors left the rendevous area and started for the lagoon entrance on parallel single files. Forty-two LVT(1)s made up the first wave with eight empty tractors following to pick up the men from amtracs that broke down or were stopped by enemy fire. The second wave of twenty-four LVT(2)s and the third of twenty-one were followed by five spares with the same mission. As additional insurance, the remaining twenty-five LVT(1)s available to

the division were still on board the transports, crammed with initial resupplies of food, water, and ammunition for the assault troops, but available in a pinch to replace troop-carrying tractors.

The scheduled H-Hour was 0830 hours, when the Marines were to hit the beaches, but it was not long before it was apparent that this time could not be met. The culprit was the strong western current which had plagued the transports earlier. While the tractors labored to keep up speed against this current, the remainder of the pre-landing drama was played.

Shortly after daybreak, the mine-sweeper *Pursuit*, followed by its sister ship *Requisite*, began clearing the lagoon passage. Smoke pots laid out by LCVPs helped to screen the sweeping operation which was helpful when Japanese shore defense guns began to seek out the two small vessels. Much more helpful was the presence of the destroyers *Ringgold* and *Dashiell* which were standing off the passage waiting to move into the lagoon. The destroyers opened up with their 5 in. guns and were able to

silence the Japanese fire. The *Pursuit*, once a lane was cleared, began marking the line of departure, boat lanes, and dangerous shoals, helped in this task by the *Maryland's* observation float plane. When the *Requisite* began to lead the destroyers into the lagoon, the Japanese shore batteries opened up again, duelling with the ships. *Ringgold* was hit twice, fortunately both times by duds, but its return fire struck home. An enormous explosion flared up ashore as a lucky shell reached an enemy ammunition dump. Again the Japanese guns fell silent.

By 0715 hours the *Pursuit* had taken up her position on the line of departure. She turned on a searchlight and aimed it seaward through the passage to guide the LVT waves through the screen of dust-laden smoke that had rolled out from the island. As she plotted the tractors' progress on radar it was obvious that they were having hard going, and the minesweeper reported to Admiral Hill that the assault waves were twenty-four minutes behind schedule. Hill's aerial observer, Lieutenant-Commander Robert Macpherson, confirmed the delay, and the admiral radioed the task force that H-Hour would be delayed until 8045 hours. When Macpherson reported that the leading wave did not cross the line of departure until 0823 hours, Hill again postponed H-Hour to 0900, since it would take at least that long for the tractors to reach the beaches.

On schedule, according to the original plan, carrier planes appeared over Betio at 0825 hours to make a last-minute strafing run over the beaches. Once the *Maryland's* guns ceased firing, the radios on the air support net were able to reach the strike commander and inform him of the change of plan. The supposed last-minute air attack took place at 0855 as rescheduled, but when it happened the tractors were still well off shore. The practical results of this attack were again questioned by the flyers themselves, one of whom declared that 'longitudinal strafing up and down the beach by fighters is not only ineffective but a mere waste of ammunition.'

The naval gunfire bombardment on the landing area was lifted inland when the planes attacked and not resumed at 0900 hours, except by the *Dashiell* and *Ringgold*, whose gunnery officers could see the landing waves. For about ten minutes the lead amtracs could rely only on the two destroyers for covering fire and on the pair of ·50 caliber machine guns that each LVT(1) had mounted on its bow. These guns opened up when the line of tractors passed the end of the long pier and ground their way over the reef's edge.

The assault troops were headed for three beaches: Red 1, which ran about 700 yards from the north-west tip of the island to a point about midway to the coastal pier, an area that included the beak and throat of the Betio bird; Red 2, the shortest beach, 600 yards long, which covered the rest of the distance to the pier; and Red 3, which stretched 800 yards from the east side of the pier to a point opposite the end of the airfield. The pier dominated the landing area and its neutralization as an enemy strongpoint was essential.

The knock-out job was given to First-Lieutenant William Hawkins and his 2nd Scout-Sniper Platoon.

Opposite: The landing beaches are hidden by smoke *Above:* Lieutenant William Hawkins, whose task was to neutralise the long pier

Hawkins' men were all expert riflemen and the thirty-year-old leader, a Texan who had been field-commissioned on Guadalcanal, was just the man to head such a special outfit. He was the first Marine to land at Betio. His LCVP, carrying half his outfit, touched down at the edge of the reef at 0855 hours as the planes were beginning their strafing runs. Hawkins, accompanied by an engineer officer, Second-Lieutenant Alan Leslie, and four of the scouts ran up the ramp leading from the reef to the top of the pier and moved amongst a pile of fuel drums that was stacked there. At first, the platoon commander signalled the rest of his men to follow him up on the pier, but when Japanese small arms fire began smacking into the drums, he waved the rest of the Marines back. The six men then moved rapidly down the pier, wiping out the few Japanese defenders and destroying any structure that might house enemy guns. Two shacks, which were set ablaze by the flamethrower Leslie carried, burned rapidly and the fire spread to the pier itself, eating its way through the planking. The resulting gap in the pier was to hinder

resupply operations later, but at this point in the proceedings it was of little consequence. Hawkins and his little group had done their job well; no enemy would use the pier to pour flanking fire into the landing waves.

With his mission accomplished, Lieutenant Hawkins left the pier, got back in his LCVP, and tried to use a boat channel that ran along the west side of pier to get to Betio. The water proved to be too shallow to float the boat over the reef, even in the channel, and Hawkin's platoon eventually reached the island after transferring to LVTs. In that they were fortunate, at least for the immediate moment, since the amtracs' light armor gave them some protection from the storm of enemy fire that was sweeping the waters off Betio. Those Marines who couldn't find an LVT to ride to shore had a never-to-be-forgotten experience – those that lived through it.

The Japanese were more than ready to take on the Marines. The intelligence had been accurate, and the preliminary bombardment largely ineffective; lots of enemy troops with lots of guns still manned the coastal

defenses. Shells burst over the tractors as they reached an area about 3,000 yards from shore and this fire continued as the evenly spaced lines moved on. As the LVTs cleared the reef edge and lumbered onto the coral surface, enemy machine gun fire slashed across the water and anti-boat guns began zeroing in on individual tractors.

The most fortunate assault battalion was the 2nd Battalion, 8th Marines. It got the major benefit from the destroyer fire coming from the lagoon which hammered Red 3 without let-up until 0910 hours. The first LVTs crawled out of the water seven minutes later and were soon followed by the faster LVT(2)s of the second and third waves. Two of the lead tractors found a break in the sea wall and continued inland until they reached the airfield taxi strip, where men of Company E rolled over the sides and took up defensive positions. The rest of Company E, Company F, and a platoon from Company G, the tractor assault element of 522 men, suffered less than twenty-five casualties in the landing. As the LVTs moved

Military police follow up to work on the beaches

back to sea, many backed off the beach to keep their armored cabs facing the shore for the Japanese were gradually recovering from the preliminary bombardment and the volume and tempo of defensive fire was picking up on the eastern beach. Inland, the Marines of 2/8 were attacking pillboxes and gun positions and the brief holiday on Red 3 was over.

Red 3 was the only place on Betio where the assault waves got ashore with ease. In the center, off Red 2, the enemy fire was lethal. Several tractors carrying men of the 2/2 were hit by artillery and anti-boat guns; dead and wounded drivers slumped over their controls and the survivors of direct hits had to jump down into the shallow water and wade in, braving the machine gun fire. For those who reached Betio in the LVTs, the beach proved no safer than the reef.

The first wave of amtracs ground ashore at 0922 hours and when the Marines poured over the sides they were immediately chewed up by small arms fire coming from the front and both flanks. Two platoons of Company E landed on the right half of Red 2 and were able to move only a short distance inland against the harrowing fire; casualties among officers and NCOs mounted alarmingly. The remaining platoon of Company E landed on the extreme left of Red 1, got over the sea wall, and knocked out a Japanese strongpoint despite its murderous fire. Then the platoon leader went down and what was left of the platoon took cover in a large shellhole.

In the left center of Red 2, Company F lost about half its strength in getting to the beach and over the sea wall. The survivors set up a series of positions held by small groups of riflemen and machine gunners about fifty yards inland. There was no contact that morning with Company E on the right; radios failed to work and runners were fair game for enemy snipers. Most of the third assault company, G, landed between the areas held by the other two, taking severe losses to reach the beach and the doubtful shelter of the log barricade.

First LVTs approach Red Beach 3. The long pier is afire after Hawkins' work

Already the narrow strip of sand was crowded with casualties, with men using the wall as a firing parapet, and with the remnants of headquarters groups trying to establish some form of control in the chaotic conditions of the first hour of fighting ashore.

Acts of courage were commonplace in the confused fighting on the beaches, but some men stood out, like Staff-Sergeant William Bordelon of Texas, an assault engineer from 1/18. His amtrac was knocked out on the run in to the beach; only four men survived the enemy shell. Bordelon led this remnant ashore and immediately made up two demolition charges and blew up two enemy pillboxes that were firing on the tractors. Attacking a third position he was hit by machine gun fire, but kept going, using a rifle to provide covering fire for other Marines scaling the sea wall. Waving away corpsmen who wanted to treat his wounds, he next raced out into the water to pick up an injured Marine who was calling for help and assisted another wounded man to reach shore as he returned to the beach. Not stopping, he prepared another demolition charge and single-handedly attacked a Japanese emplacement. This time the enemy gunners cut the incre-

dible sergeant down. He was post-humously awarded the Medal of Honor, the first of four Marines of the 2nd Division to win their nation's highest decoration at Tarawa.

A complex of Japanese emplacements bristling with anti-boat and machine guns located near the Red 1–Red 2 boundary was one of the principal causes of a disorganized landing on Red 1 by the 3rd Battalion, 2nd Marines. Company K, the left assault unit, was particularly hard hit; a number of its tractors were knocked out and the men were cut to pieces as they waded to shore. On the right, Company I, landing at about 0910 hours, was not hit as hard in the water, but many of its men, including the company commander, were killed as the attack pressed inland. Fire was coming from the strongpoints on the left flank, from enemy positions to the front, and from Green Beach, the western end of the island. Losses mounted alarmingly but some unexpected reinforcements came ashore behind the assault waves. The devastating fire from the Japanese position on the beach boundary drove the LVTs

Marines wade ashore. Most faced withering fire during the 500 yard walk

carrying a platoon of Company G of 2/2 to land on the right of Red 1, where they joined the furious battle.

In each of the landing formations, the battalion commander and part of his headquarters group was in a free boat between the third and fourth waves, ready to land as circumstances warranted. Each of these men reached Betio in a different way illustrative of the grim morning's proceedings. One came ashore unscathed, another was brought in by a burial detail, and the third landed on the wrong beach and did not reach his unit on D-Day.

Off Red 3, Major Henry 'Jim' Crowe, an ex-enlisted man with a bushy red mustache and a bull bellow, saw that his LCM could not make it to the beach and didn't wait for an LVT to come back and pick him up. Ordering his coxswain to lower the boat's ramp and his own men to spread out, the major led his headquarters group to the beach and with characteristic nerve, he reached Red 3 only four minutes behind the third assault wave of LVT(2)s. Enemy fire was not yet heavy on Red 3, thanks to the destroyers, but Crowe's group was the last that would wade or ride in without being cut to pieces by Japanese fire.

Lieutenant-Colonel Herbert Amey, a

The LCM (Landing Craft Mechanised) II. Not being an amphibious craft, the LCM II was much hampered by the reefs that bedevilled the landings on Betio. It was however a useful and versatile landing craft, capable of carrying a vehicle or a light tank. *Weight:* 20 tons. *Length:* 45 feet. *Beam:* 14 feet 1 inch. *Engines:* Two 100 horse power petrol engines. *Speed:* $7\frac{1}{2}$ knots. *Range:* 75 miles. *Crew:* 4. *Payload:* One vehicle or light tank. *Armament:* One or two .5 Browning machine guns

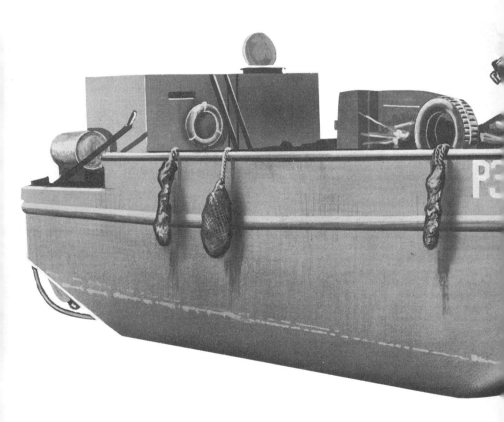

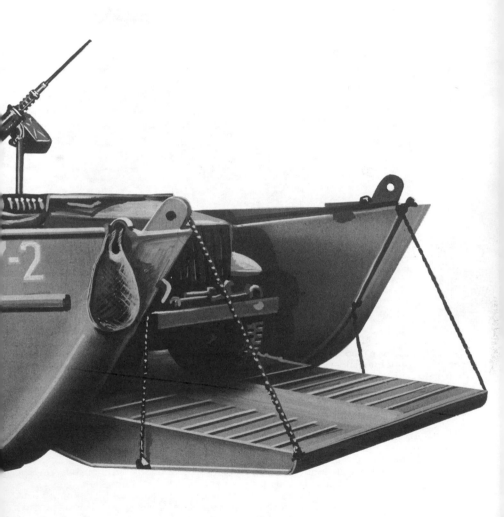

**Major 'Jim' Crowe, second
from right, and his officers consult
their map**

tall, handsome officer who commanded
2/2, was killed as he strove to reach
Betio. He had hailed two LVTs re-
turning from the beach and transferred his headquarters element to
them. Then, when his tractor was
about 200 yards from land, it was
stopped by a tangle of barbed wire and
everyone, about fifteen officers and
men, dismounted for the dangerous
walk. A fusillade of machine gun fire
cut Amey down and with him three
others; the remainder slogged ahead
to the shelter of a wrecked boat where
Lieutenant-Colonel Walter Jordan,
an observer from the 4th Marine
Division and the senior officer present,
announced that he was taking command until the battalion executive
officer, Major Howard Rice, could get
ashore. Forging ahead again despite
the deadly fire, Jordon's group reached
the beach at about 1000 hours and set
up shop in a shell hole amid the
awesome scene of carnage and destruction. The headquarters radios
were all out of action, damaged by
enemy fire or by immersion in sea
water. When runners from the three
rifle companies found the command
group, the messages all were grim;
they added up to news of crippling
casualties, little forward progress,
and no connected front.

The situation on Red 1 was a little
brighter than it was on the center
beach, but none of the senior commanders knew it. Again the salt water

had played havoc with the battalion radios and contact with the rest of the division was sporadic at best. This didn't deter the officer who ended up commanding the troops on the northwest tip of Betio. Major Michael Ryan led Company L which made up most of the fourth wave. As his boat approached the reef, he saw that it was littered with holed and smoking tractors, most of them to the left of the landing area where Company K had gone in. Some men were standing up and moving inland on the right section of the beach near the beak of the island. Ryan therefore directed the landing craft to bear to the right, to the west of the hulk of a wrecked Japanese ship that lay on the reef, and to head for the beach.

The LCVPs grounded on the coral about 500 yards from shore, and the men began the long walk as Japanese shells exploded in their midst and machine gun fire raked the ragged lines. The major commandeered an LVT coming back from the beach, climbed aboard, and headed it back to land. When he jumped down on Betio and looked back, all he could see was heads with rifles held over them. Many of his men, wanting to make themselves as small a target as possible, were crouched low in the water but they were still coming on. About 100-150 yards out the reef shelved upward and the water offered little concealment. Here the men picked up the pace a bit, but there was no respite from enemy fire and Marines were dropping on every hand. By the time Company L and its attached 81mm mortar platoon reached shore, the fourth wave had suffered thirty five per cent casualties.

The battalion commander of the 3/2, Major John Schoettel, was busy while Ryan and his men were moving ashore. He spotted some LCMs, which were carrying medium tanks intended for Red 1, starting to turn away from the reef edge and he ordered them to reverse course and land the tanks. Then, as the mediums were carefully following guides to the beach, Schoettel assessed the situation for the remainder of his battalion still waiting in boats offshore. Few LVTs were coming back from Red 1; the long stretch of water off the beach was dotted with wrecked vehicles, and dead Marines floated aimlessly everywhere. The Japanese fire was obviously exacting a murderous toll from Ryan's men for their passage. Under the circumstances, Major Schoettel decided to hold up landing the rest of the 3rd Battalion.

At 0959 hours, Schoettel radioed Shoup: 'Troops held up on reef on right flank of Red 1; troops receiving heavy fire in water.' Shoup replied: 'Land Red 2 and work west.' The answer was a discouraging: 'We have nothing left to land.' For several hours, Schoettel and his remaining men stayed off the reef, while the only troops to reach Red 1 alive were those in tractors who were driven west from the Red 2 landing lanes by the fire of the strongpoints at the juncture of Red 1 and 2. Finally, at 1458, when Major Schoettel reported that he was out of contact with his assault units and had still not landed the rest of his battalion, the division commander took a hand in the message traffic, directing the 3/2 commander to 'land at any cost, regain control of your battalion, and continue the attack.' Schoettel and his men, following Colonel Shoup's earlier orders, got ashore on Red 2 late that evening.

This byplay had little effect on the course of operations ashore, but it did heighten the anxiety about 3/2's fate. The lack of radio contact with the western beachhead – for there were two distinct beachheads on Betio – was not uncommon elsewhere on the island. The Marine radios were low-power sets, the TBX and TBY; the first had little range and the other frequently failed when it got wet. So there were many times ashore when the only means of communication were runners or wire, and both the messengers and the wiremen were fair game for enemy snipers and machine gunners. Offshore, the commanders were often mystified about what was going on on Betio; the reports of aerial observers were useful, but they could not tell General Smith or Admiral Hill who was doing the things that they saw. As a consequence, a steady stream of officer messengers and observers were sent ashore to find out what was going on.

Enough of the radio messages concerning the situation ashore got through, however, for Colonel Shoup to take charge of the assault operations as he was trying his own luck at landing on Betio. The 2nd Combat Team headquarters group, embarked in an LCVP, reached the reef near the pier as turn-around amtracs were coming out from the beaches. Hailing an LVT that was carrying casualties from Red 2 to the transports, Shoup had the wounded Marines transferred to his boat. He then boarded the tractor, taking with him a small staff that included his operations officer and the regimental surgeon, an observer, Lieutenant-Colonel Evans Carlson, and the commanding officer of the team's artillery battalion (1/10), Lieutenant-Colonel Presley Rixey.

After an abortive attempt to land on Red 3 that was turned back by heavy enemy fire, Shoup's LVT headed for the center beach. The Japanese were just as unwilling to have the tractor land on Red 2. A hail of shell fragments ripped at the amtrac's occupants, and then half-way to the beach, Shoup recalled, 'a kid named White was shot, the LVT was holed, and the driver went into the water.' With the amtrac stalled, the colonel said, 'Let's get out of here,' and suiting actions to words led the command group over the side. The party waded to the shelter of the pier, which was a frame structure with occasional sections of coral rock fill which offered some cover from the deadly Japanese guns.

It was while he was proceeding towards Betio that Shoup, at 0958

Reinforcement waves come ashore alongside the pier

hours, ordered his reserve battalion, the 1/2, to land on Red 2. When this unit, commanded by Major Wood Kyle, reached the reef about 1030 hours, a naval boat flotilla commander told him that no landing craft could reach the island and that his men would have to transfer to tractors. Enough LVTs had survived the initial landing and return across the fire-swept water to load Companies A and B. Company C eventually found enough tractors about noon to make its run in, but there were no LVTs for the rest of the battalion. Headquarters Company was left in its boats under the battalion executive officer to come ashore as soon as it could. Even though Kyle was fortunate enough to garner enough amtracs to land his rifle companies, they were not spared the effects of the continuous enemy

Major Robert H. Ruud, commander of
3rd Battalion, 8th Marines

Major Michael Ryan, leader of
Company L of Landing Team One

fusillade. Some LVTs were hit, and the units in them were decimated as they waded to the beach.

Again the defensive complex at the right flank of Red 2 produced fire so heavy and accurate that it broke up the landing formations and forced tractors carrying a good part of the 1st Battalion, four officers and 110 men, to shift west to land in Major Ryan's beachhead. Since the Japanese position was already responsible for sending him one rifle and two machine gun platoons from the 2/2, by the same route and for the same reason, the commander on Red 1 could, by twisted logic, be thankful to the enemy gunners. His own battalion had suffered so many casualties, almost fifty per cent among assault units during the morning's fighting, that any and all reinforcements were welcome.

The matter of reinforcements concerned the division commander too. Soon after Colonel Shoup committed Major Kyle's battalion, General Smith ordered Colonel Elmer Hall, commanding the 8th Marines, to send his 3rd Battalion to the line of departure to report to Shoup. At 1103 hours,

when 3/8's commander, Major Robert H Ruud, contacted the colonel, he was ordered to land his unit in support on Major Crowe's battalion. There were no tractors available when Ruud's first waves reached the reef, and the Marines of Companies K and L stepped off the ramps of their boats to brave the barrier of enemy fire. Even as the Japanese began to find their marks, some of the men, heavily laden with combat gear, stepped into deep holes in the reef and were dragged under, drowned before they were shot.

For the rest of the men in the two companies, the long, 700-yard walk through shoulder-high, then chest-high, waist-high, and knee-high water was horrible and never forgotten. Shoup and his staff from their position at the pier could see the terrible carnage and waved to the nearest men of 3/8 to come over to the pier and its partial cover. Some Marines saw the frantically waving officers and reached the pier, thoroughly shaken by their experience. The rest trudged onward toward the beach, pushing their way through water tinged with blood and whipped by shell explosions and criss-crossing lines of machine gun fire. Bodies and parts of bodies lay everywhere; the wounded who could walk alone staggered on, those who were hurt too badly were helped by the men nearest to them, men who were often hit themselves before they reached the shore. Only about one hundred men, thirty per cent of the first wave, got to Betio in one piece.

The Marines in the second and third waves of Ruud's outfit could see what was happening as they too started for shore. Their commanders decided to move in along the pier and the boats unloaded there. As the men walked along the trestles, some of them moved under the pier to the Red 2 side, but the enemy fire was just as strong there. Major Ruud, who had lost radio contact with Colonel Shoup, reported to Colonel Hall that his third wave was 'practically wiped out' in its landing and that his fourth wave had pulled away from the pier's end after unloading a few men. The Japanese, attracted by the tempting target of the milling boats, had concentrated their fire on the pier and the fourth wave was considerably disorganized. As Ruud withdrew the boats out of range of small arms fire to regroup, he received a message from the assistant division commander (ADC), Brigadier-General Leo Hermle, who was on board the transport *Monrovia* with Colonel Hall, to 'land no further troops until directed.'

Colonel Shoup, at this point shortly before noon, had reached Betio and selected a command post (CP) site near the center of the Marine-held portion of Red 2. His headquarters was located on the beach side of a big sand-covered Japanese bunker which afforded some shelter from enemy fire. The combat team commander was now better able to take stock of what was happening on Betio and the picture he assembled was not an encouraging one. Major Crowe's 2/8 seemed to be in the best shape; it held the most territory, with forward positions near the airfield and his men in some places nearly 200 yards inland. Lieutenant-Colonel Jordan, whom Shoup had ordered to retain command of the 2/2, could report that his Marines had a tenuous hold on a beachhead of scattered positions no more than 75 yards deep, a fact that the regimental commander could easily verify since his CP was repeatedly the target of sniper fire. As for the 3/2, Shoup knew from reports that he had received from Schoettel and from messages that got through from the *Maryland* that Marines were ashore on the western part of the island. That's about all he knew of his 3rd Battalion's situation.

The two reinforcing battalions which were landing in increments all through the mid-day period were sorely needed. Kyle's men were fed into the frontlines near the pier to the left of the 2/2 as soon as they reached shore. As the Marines of the 3/8 came trickling in, they immediately came under the command of Major Crowe who used them to bolster his own lines. In many instances the late arrivals were in worse shape that the original assault troops, had suffered heavier casualties, and were more disrupted by the scattering of units in the landings.

Despite the touch-and-go nature of the fighting and his severe personnel losses, there was a tough confidence exuded by Shoup that pervaded his CP. At 1230 hours, not trusting the erratic radios which had already failed him often, the colonel resolved to send an officer back to the command ship to give the division and attack force commanders a first-hand account of the Marine situation on Bieto and to explain the plan he had formulated to capture the island – to attack south and west to unite the two beachheads before attempting to seize the eastern end. Not knowing how the battle was faring on Red 1, he wanted any available reserves landed on Red 2 where he could use them to best advantage. He chose Lieutenant Colonel Carlson to explain the situation to those on the *Maryland* and added: 'You tell the general and the admiral that we are going to stick and fight it out.'

A toehold gained

While Carlson was making his way out to the command ship, General Smith was digesting the fragmentary reports he had received from shore and the word he got from aerial observers. Since the battleship was the communication hub of the operation, he was in a good position to assess what could be done to help Shoup. With the commitment of the 3/8, the general had only one infantry battalion in reserve and it too was standing by to land. Colonel Hall had received orders to boat the remainder of his combat team soon after 3/8 reported to Shoup. Regimental headquarters and the 1st Battalion were ordered to move to the line of departure at 1343 hours.

Twelve minutes earlier, after he had reported the situation at Betio to General Holland Smith, the 2nd Division commander had asked that the corps reserve, the 6th Combat Team, be released to his control. While he awaited a reply, Julian Smith had his staff working on a plan to organize the remaining division support troops, communicators, clerks, engineers, and artillerymen, into provisional infantry battalions to be used in the fighting ashore. This drastic plan, which illustrated the desperate nature of the battle on D-Day, proved unnecessary. In less than an hour after he had asked for the reserves, Smith received his answer from Admiral Turner. The 6th Marines were returned to 2nd Division command.

Now the general could take the risk of landing 1/8. He sent a message to Colonel Shoup asking him where he should land the battalion, on Beach Green (the western end of the island) or on Red 2 and 3, and if a night landing of reinforcements was practical. The commander ashore never received the message. The communications failures continued. Later in the afternoon, as the men of Colonel Hall's group waited at the line of departure, 'cramped, wet, hungry, tired, and a large number . . . seasick', the division ordered the colonel to make an assault landing on the extreme eastern end of the island and attack north-west towards Shoup's beachhead. Again the word never reached the man for whom it was intended. The 8th Marines elements spend the remainder of the day and all night in the open boats

waiting for orders that never came.

The division commander, anxious to see how the new plan of attack would work, sent his logistics officer, Lieutenant-Colonel Jesse Cook, aloft as an observer in a *Maryland* scout plane. Cook was to report the movement of 1/8 from the line of departure, and when he radioed back that a number of boats were moving towards Red 2, there was consternation in the division command post. Hall was landing on the wrong beach! But he wasn't. What Cook had seen was the LCVPs carrying the artillery batteries of 1/10 towards Betio. It was midnight before the truth finally filtered through the tangled communication channels and the combat team headquarters and its single battalion were correctly located on division operations maps, still at the line of departure and not ashore on Red 2.

The assistant division commander, General Hermle, was also a victim of the on-again, off-again radio traffic. Since General Smith, like Colonel Shoup, was anxious to clarify the situation ashore, he ordered Hermle to

Above: Brigadier-General Leo D Hermle, assistant divisional commander. *Opposite:* A tank follows the marines ashore on Red Beach 3

proceed to the end of the long pier, size up the situation, and report his findings back to the *Maryland*. After leaving the *Monrovia* with his staff, Hermle tried to contact Shoup and pinpoint the location of his CP, but he could not raise the 2nd Combat Team commander. When the ADC did reach the pier at 1740 hours, he reported that area was under enemy fire. Then, when he tried to raise the *Maryland* again to report what news he had of the action ashore, his radios got no response. He sent a messenger with this information out to the nearest ship so it could be relayed to the flagship. Meanwhile, he busied himself with squaring away the confusion at the pier's end and helped start carrying parties and reinforcements towards shore.

It was early on the morning of D-plus 1 before Hermle broke away from the pier and moved with his staff

to the *Pursuit* in order to use its radio
and inform General Smith that
Colonel Shoup wanted 1/8 to land on
Red 2. After this message was sent at
0445 hours, the ADC was abruptly
ordered to report to the division
commander. When he reached the
Maryland, Hermle found the usually
benign Smith quite perturbed. It
seems that he had ordered Hermle to
take command of all troops ashore at
1750 hours the previous evening and to
report when he had an advance division CP set up. Then, throughout the
night there had been no word of the
fate of the ADC group. Once it became
apparent that Hermle had not dis-
obeyed his orders and was not a casu-
ality, the atmosphere cleared. The up-
shot of this particular communication
failure, however, was that Shoup
remained in command on Betio on 21st
November.

Although the 1st Battalion, 8th
Marines could have been used ashore
on D-Day, it is doubtful if it would
have made it to the beach as a coher-
ent unit. Very few battalions did. Only
Major Crowe was lucky enough to
get most of his men on Betio in organized and familiar formations that were
not torn apart by landing casualties.
As a consequence, 2/8 was a bulwark
of Shoup's beachhead and the colonel
relied heavily on Crowe and his men.

Perhaps the biggest boon to the men
of the 8th Marines was the safe arrival
of several Sherman medium tanks on
their beach during the early hours of
the D-Day action. Scheduled to land
on Red 3 shortly after H-Hour were the
2d and 3d Platoons of Company C, I
Marine Amphibious Corps Tank Battalion, a unit that foresightedly had
been attached to the Tarawa assault
forces. The 2d Division's own tank
companies were equipped with light
tanks whose main armament was a
37mm gun, an excellent weapon against
personnel but virtually useless in an
attack on the enemy's concrete and
steel bunkers. The Shermans' 75mm
guns packed a close-range wallop
that could knock out the smaller
Japanese emplacements.

Although no guides were available

**Wounded but still fighting, a marine
leads the way round a beach
entanglement**

off Red 3 to lead the mediums across the reef, seven tanks threaded their way through the shellholes and wrecked amtracs safely; only one was lost when it plunged into an unseen depression. Finding a break in the seawall, the four tanks of the 3d Platoon reported to Major Crowe about 1130 hours. About the same time, three tanks of the 2d Platoon turned west toward Red 2 to find Colonel Shoup.

Crowe immediately put his Shermans to use, adding their punch to the drive to the south and east by 2/8 and the bits and pieces of 3/8 that had reached shore. In its first hour of battle, one Sherman was knocked out by a dive bomber as it was working forward of the lines in the area being hit by air and naval gunfire support. In short order, two more tanks were aflame and abandoned, one when it blundered into a pit crowded with fuel drums, which were promptly set afire by the bombers, and the other when it was wrecked by Japanese gunfire. The remaining tank, although hit repeatedly by enemy gunners, remained in action, moving to the left flank of Crowe's position where strong resistance was centered on a steel pillbox and a large concrete bunker near the end of the Burns-Philp pier.

This pier, named after the British company that had exported copra from the Gilberts in pre-war years, extended 200 feet out onto the reef. It marked the eastern limit of Crowe's holdings on D-Day, a point about 400 yards from the long pier at the Red 2-Red 3 boundary. Company F of 2/8, which initially worked against the defenses near the Burns-Philp pier, had suffered heavy casualties from Japanese grenades when it was pinned down by machine gun fire. Crowe ordered Company G over to reinforce F and moved what was left of Company K of 3/88 into position to the right, where it joined its lines to those of Company E. Company E had moved into the triangle formed by the east and west taxistrips of the island's airfield. About thirty-five men from

Holed up behind flimsy cover on Red Beach 3, the marines prepare to move towards the Burns Philp pier

Companies I and L of 3/8, all that had got ashore by mid-afternoon, were used to outpost the right flank of the position in the triangle. Later, when Major Ruud got ashore, this group was doubled in strength.

With naval guns pounding the eastern end of the island and carrier planes hitting the Japanese defenses on the ocean shore, there was a ring of flame and explosions around Major

Crowe's perimeter. The impact area, however, was several hundred yards from the small groups of Marines taking cover in shellholes and the confusing tangle of debris that littered the island. Close in, the Japanese were free to meet the Americans head on, and the enemy positions could only be taken by close-quarter fighting.

In an attempt to advance east down the lagoon shore, the engineer flamethrower and demolition teams attached to 2/8, led by First Lieutenant Alexánder Bonnyman, worked on the

A unit takes cover in the debris while the machine gunner goes into action

south entrance to the big bunker forward of Company F's lines. At the same time, an infantry platoon tried to move past its south flank. Machine gun fire from the steel pill box to the left and from other positions to the front practically wiped out the platoon. This loss prompted a decision by Crowe to hold what he had in this area and stand fast.

Further inland, Company K of 3/8, menaced by a Japanese tank that could be seen maneuvering near the end of the eastern taxiway, managed to manhandle two 37mm guns up to its lines. The fire of these guns drove off the tank, which disappeared into the tangle of undergrowth, twisted and battered trees, and half-seen structures that characterized the eastern end of Betio. The 37s also scattered a group of 100–200 Japanese, who were spotted moving through the brush from the south to the north shore during the afternoon. After these incidents, the guns were incorporated into the frontline defenses and most efforts were bent toward building up strength on the perimeter for the fast-approaching night.

The 8th Marines' reinforcements for Red 3, Major Ruud's 3rd Battalion, continued to come in during the afternoon. Ruud made radio contact with Crowe about 1400 hours and the 2/8 commander briefed him on the situation ashore. After Ruud went to the *Pursuit* to fill Colonel Hall in on the picture of what was happening to his men on Betio, the major returned to his troops and at 1500 hours was ordered by Colonel Shoup to land the rest of his battalion, coming in along the west side of the long pier. During the next several hours, the Marines came ashore by any means possible, in LVTs when they could find space in them, but mostly on foot. With Shoup's permission, Lieutenant-Colonel Carlson delayed his trip out to the *Maryland* and diverted his amtrac to the pier to load and land several groups of Marines from 3/8, who had taken shelter from the unceasing enemy fire under and alongside the structure. Major Ruud led some of his men to shore and left his executive officer at the pier's end to organize and send in anyone else he could find from the boat teams that had been scattered and driven to cover as soon as they set foot on the reef.

On Betio Major Ruud reported to Colonel Shoup and was ordered to reorganize Companies I and L of his battalion, taking up defensive positions in the airfield triangle directly inland from the long pier. Ruud's Company K was by now so integrated into the defenses of 2/8 that it remained under Crowe's command for the rest of struggle to capture the island.

In the center of Shoup's beachhead, the landing of Major Kyle's battalion gave the colonel a chance to extend his lines inland and get some breathing space near the beach. Companies A and B of the 1/2 had been hard hit during their landing, but the survivors pushed inland wherever their tractors put them ashore with most of them bunched in an area within 150–200 yards of the pier. About twenty five men from Company A, led by their company commander, advanced to the edge of the western taxistrip before enemy fire drove them back. Like the Marines of the 2/2, those of the 1st Battalion then started the dangerous

and seemingly unending process of destroying Japanese defensive positions one by one. In a process that one senior Army general was later to describe aptly as the 'blowtorch and corkscrew' method, engineer teams with flamethrowers, satchel charges, and bangalore torpedoes attempted to kill the Japanese by searing the firing ports of emplacements with flame while demolitions were placed to seal all openings. Infantry covering fire was an essential part of this teamwork. The cost of such attacks was high; there was virtually no way to approach the mutually-supporting defensive positions without being nakedly exposed to enemy fire. Once a breach was made, however, the way was open for a tiny advance, but the pace was painfully slow and the destruction drama had to be played over and over again without any end to the casualties. Until the band of coastal defenses was eliminated, no one could walk upright with impunity on Betio. The usual stance on D-Day was a low crouch in the lee of the four-foot-high sea wall and a crawl anywhere inland. The assault troops knew that the Japanese were looking right down their throats and yet there was always someone ready to lead an attack and others to follow. Courage on Betio was so commonplace that many fantastic acts of heroism and self-sacrifice went unnoticed in the general sharing of danger.

Three of the Shermans that had landed on Red 3 reported to Colonel Shoup about noon and he sent them west to attempt to break through to the 3/2 on Red 1. As they approached the enemy strongpoint complex on the beach boundary, the Marines, strung out along the right flank in any position that offered them cover, waved the mediums back. The defending fire was too strong even for the Shermans. When the tank platoon shifted to the left to help Marines cross the west taxistrip, it suffered much the same fate as the platoon on Red 3. One medium plunged into a deep shellhole and had to be abandoned; another was disabled by a mine. The survivor kept

First-Lieutenant Alexander Bonnyman won the Medal of Honor at Tarawa

68

fighting, attacking close-in emplacements at point-blank range and shelling the ones further out from which enemy fire was raking the Marines.

The attack across the taxistrip was part of a general advance ordered by Colonel Shoup at 1400 hours. Major Kyle had landed and taken command of his battalion about 1330 hours and he and Lieutenant Colonel Jordon were directed to drive toward the south shore of the island. Jordan's battalion, with many of its infantry and heavy weapons squads either knocked out or driven ashore on Red 1, was grossly understrength. He could do little more than consolidate his hold on the right flank of the beachhead. Kyle was able to advance Company B into the taxistrip triangle; Company A joined it there and tied in on the right and Company C extended the line back toward the beach. These gains were made only after hours of furious small unit battles that left the survivors exhausted but still strong enough and wise enough to dig in as dusk approached. On the extreme right flank, what was left of the 2/2 held a tenuous line with fifty-seven men from four companies occupying the forward positions.

Despite the severe casualties tnat the four battalions in Shoup's beachhead had suffered in getting ashore and establishing a toehold on the island, there was no sense of panic in the lines as the Marines set up for night defense. Stragglers kept appearing from the beach; here, an 81mm mortar squad lugging its heavy loads of tube, base plate, and ammunition; there, a machine gun and its crew or a small group of riflemen. These Marines were fed into the lines wherever a gap occurred, and there were many, or they were pulled together into makeshift reserve forces without much regard to what unit they might have belonged to. There might be time to sort everyone out the next day; but at dusk on 20th November the business at hand was to see that there were Marines on Betio the next day.

The battle of Red 1, like that on the central beachhead, was also influenced by the landing of medium tanks on the morning of D-Day. After Major Schoettel turned the LCMs back to the reef, the boats

unloaded the 30 ton Shermans on the edge of the coral shelf. Guides carrying flags to mark holes in the reef preceded the six tanks, wading through more than 1,000 yards of water and taking casualties as enemy machine gunners found the unprotected men easy targets. When the mediums approached the beach, they found the narrow strip of sand crowded with dead and wounded Marines. The tank group commander, unwilling to take the risk of threading his way through the casualties, led his Shermans west around the beak of Betio to a position off Green Beach. It was during this detour that four of the tanks lunged into holes and drowned out; the two remaining then moved inland through a breach in the seawall blasted by engineers.

Major Ryan welcomed the Shermans' firepower and crushing action and put them to work shooting up the Green Beach defenses. The major had decided that he did not have enough men to sweep the length of Red 1 and was going to concentrate on securing Green Beach. As the senior officer of 3/2 shore, he had taken command of the battalion when he and the other company commanders decided that it was highly improbable that anyone from the headquarters units would be able to get through the Japanese fire off Red 1. About 1400 hours, Ryan organized an attack to the south and put his two tanks out in front to lead the way. The battalion 81mm mortars furnished suppressive fire, and the men, surpisingly, were able to advance, taking successive Japanese positions from the flank.

The enemy fire was heavy and accurate. One tank was knocked out of action and set afire; the remaining Sherman had its turret and 75mm gun immobilized by a crippling hit, but the bow machine gun was still active and was used to provide covering fire for the infantry. The attack was continually frustrated by the shortage of flamethrower fuel and demolitions, for the loads the engineers had carried

Top: **Death in a pillbox. Marines have pinned down one of the defenders.** *Right:* **Unit under fire. The effect of the bombardment can be seen among the palm trees**

The Japanese Type 92 7.7mm Machine Gun.
Weight: 122 pounds with tripod. *Length:* 45.5 inches. *Ammunition:* Belts of 30 rounds each. *Rate of fire:* 450-500 rounds-per-minute. *Muzzle velocity:* 2,400 feet-per-second

ashore were quickly used up. Despite this handicap, the Marines overran many enemy positions, reaching an anti-tank ditch 300 yards from the southern shore, but they could not destroy the emplacements they had bypassed. Carrying parties and stretcher bearers were fired on continually as they made their way to and from Red 1. The volume of enemy defending fire grew more intense with every foot the Marines moved forward. Convinced that his men were over-extended and that the Japanese would counterattack, Major Ryan pulled in his assault units and fell back to a beachhead perimeter about 300 yards deep and 150 yards wide. At 1800 hours, in response to a radio message from Colonel Shoup, he reported his night defensive position, but did not mention the day's advance. Like many such messages, this one did not reach Shoup, and the combat team commander was still unsure of the situation on Red 1.

The radio Ryan used was one brought ashore by Major Rice, the executive officer of the 2/2, who had been driven ashore on Red 1 like so many others destined for Red 2. Some but not all of these men were absorbed by Ryan into his defensive perimeter; he had been so busy directing the attack

inland that he had only a general idea of the number of men and variety of units that had landed on Red 1. Actually, he had the remnants of three rifle companies and one machine gun platoon from his own battalion; two rifle platoons and two machine gun platoons from the 2/2; and about one hundred men from the 1/2. In addition to these men, there were a number of dismounted tank and amtrac crewmen, some heavy weapons crews that had lost their pieces coming ashore, some spare engineers and communicators, and a variety of other specialists, most of whom were christened infantrymen and used as combat replacements as the critical need for men arose. Everyone in the northwest corner of Betio, whether he was on Ryan's front line or on the beach, dug in as darkness fell in order to meet the universally expected counterattack.

In order to supplement the meager supplies of ammunition, rations, and water he had after a day's fighting, Major Ryan sent men out on the reef to strip the wrecked tractors of anything useful. A few undamaged LVTs with vitally-needed replenishment supplies did reach Red 1 after dark, but for the most part Ryan's collection of assorted units had to make do

Support troops pile up supplies, ammunition and medical equipment to consolidate the beachhead

with what they had. The steadily dwindling supply of tractors had been concentrated in resupply operations to Red 2.

The boat channel alongside the pier, which offered some protection to the precious tractors, was the prime route of approach to both Red 2 and 3 for both men and supplies, after the 3/8 and 1/2 had put their first waves ashore. The expenditure rate of all types of ammunition was very high in a battle as savagely-fought as that for Betio and the need for constant resupply was critical. Medical supplies, particularly blood plasma, were often scarce as seriously wounded men

were carried back to beach aid stations in such numbers that the doctors and corpsmen were hard put to keep up with the flow. There were many other resupply items that had to reach Betio, batteries for dead radios; water to replenish the two canteens that each man had carried ashore; enormous quantities of demolitions; fuel for flamethrowers; the list was endless. And all of it had to funnel down the side of the pier.

When General Hermle reached the end of the pier in the waning hours of the afternoon, the scene was chaotic. Boats were milling around off the reef waiting for a chance to dash in and unload on the pierhead or marry up with an LVT, trading supplies for casualties. Scores of men were huddled under the pier or hugging its sides; a few staunch souls were ignoring the intermittent enemy fire and trying to speed the unloading process or rounding up small groups of Marines to make a try for the beach. The general immediately took charge of the resupply and reinforcement efforts. He used his own staff and Major Stanley Larsen, executive officer of the 3/8, to organize carrying parties of infantrymen to help clear the jam of ammunition boxes, water cans, and shells. Intermittent contact with Colonel Shoup let him know what was needed most ashore, and these were items that were loaded in the LVTs and given to the human packhorses.

Earlier in the day, eager coxswains from the transports and cargo vessels, spurred on by Captain Knowles' pre-landing instructions to 'keep the boats moving and get the stuff to the Marines', had brought in whatever was loaded in their LCVPs. And the tractor crews, using any help they could find at the reef's edge, had

brought in this gear, just as convinced it was needed ashore. At sea, the ship commanders, anxious to clear their holds in these dangerous waters, had unloaded a miscellany of equipment, weapons, and supplies that had little relation to the material that Colonel Shoup found he needed. More than a little annoyed by this experience, the colonel was to become a strong advocate of letting the commander ashore determine what should be landed.

General Hermle, in order to get a first-hand account of what was happening on Betio and to find where Colonel Shoup wanted reinforcements landed, sent Major Rathvon Tompkins and Captain Thomas Dutton in to Red 2 about 1930 hours. Like the Marines struggling with their loads and weapons, the two officers had a difficult time finding their way to the beach. Japanese machine gun and anti-boat gun fire had not slackened much with darkness and a new threat had been added, since bullets were hitting among the files of men that obviously came from positions offshore. Some enemy snipers had moved out on the reef to occupy the low-lying ship hulk which stood off the right end of Red 2

Supply build-up across Red Beach 3

and others had found firing positions in the wrecked amtracs that were scattered all over the reef.

Despite the wealth of defending fire and the variety of angles from which it came, the curtain of darkness saved the lives of many Marines who came ashore on the night of 20th–21st November. Some men were even emboldened to speed their trip to shore by climbing up on the pier, but the white coral grit surface silhouetted their figures and the attention they drew from alert Japanese gunners discouraged this experiment. There was no fast way to reach Betio when you were afoot; you had to drag yourself through the water. When many of the Marines from the carrying parties reached shore, they dumped their loads and if no one stopped them they had a tendency to stay where they were, slumping exhausted against any open spot they could find on the sea wall. Remembering this scene with a professional soldier's eye Major Tompkins was struck by the inviting target it presented; he wondered why the Japanese 'didn't use mortars on the first night. People were lying on the beach so thick you couldn't walk. All they had to do was fire at the water's edge and they would have killed hundreds of Marines.'

But the Japanese didn't fire their mortars. And they didn't launch a counterattack, a fact that puzzled nearly every Marine ashore. The American situation was precarious and the Japanese still had a sizeable garrison on Betio with which to launch an attack. Reflection on this welcome omission led most Marine leaders in the battle to conclude that enemy wire communications had been destroyed in the preliminary bombardment. There appeared to be no radios at small unit levels and the Japanese naval troops evidently made little use of messengers. No field message blanks were found on Betio, although they had been captured frequently in previous operations. It appeared that Admiral Shibasaki was not able to mount a coordinated counterattack, but then that may not have been what he intended. Holed up in their formidable defenses, the Japanese were more dangerous than they might have been charging into Marine gunfire.

The gradual buildup of supplies was matched by an increase in Marine firepower too. Lieutenant-Colonel Rixey and Colonel Shoup had decided to land Rixey's pack howitzers on Red 2 instead of Red 1, where the original landing plans had called for them to go ashore. A gun section each from Batteries A and B of 1/10 were transferred to LVTs and reached the beach without mishap. Three other sections from Battery C, which received the word to land before their guns were transferred to tractors, had to' manhandle their weapons across the reef. None of the packs reached Betio until after dark and all stayed near the beach to await first light so they could register.

Once they had been briefed by Colonel Shoup, Major Tomkins and Captain Dutton began the tortuous journey out to the pier's end to report to General Hermle. Toward midnight the moon rose and its light made the trip through the exposed areas near the pier even more unpleasant than the trip shoreward had been. It was 0345 hours before the two officers found the ADC and gave him their news, and it was shortly after this that Hermle went out to the *Pursuit* to contact division headquarters, leaving the logistics officer of his staff, Lieutenant-Colonel Cliff Atkinson, to control the movement of supplies toward shore.

The Japanese made one futile gesture during the night. About eight enemy planes came over the island and dropped three sticks of bombs. The Marines waiting quietly in their foxholes for the enemy infantry to appear were treated to the sight of vivid explosions from the bombing erupting in territory held by the Japanese. It was this quiet waiting that struck experienced observers most vividly about the first night on Betio. Despite that fact that many of the small groups of Marines that manned the far-from-solid perimeters were strangers to each other and to their leaders, there was remarkable fire discipline. It was as if the men of the division had forged a tremendous unspoken confidence in themselves during the day's trials on the reefs and beaches of Betio.

Aftermath of the attack. Red
Beach 2 is littered with LVTs, weapons,
supplies, and grounded tanks in the
background

D-Plus One

Once the division staff on the *Maryland* was aware of the location of 1/8, following a report by Colonel Hall that his men were 'resting easy' in their boats near the *Pursuit,* the scheme of landing on the eastern end of Betio was revived. The 8th Marines commander was directed to arrange with Navy control officers for a new line of departure off the eastern beaches and to make other preparations for a landing at 0900 hours. Soon thereafter General Hermle's report that Colonel Shoup wanted the reserve battalion landed on Red 2 cancelled the plans for the assault on the island's tail. Instead, Hall received orders to land 1/8 immediately on Red 2; once the troops were ashore they were to attack west toward Ryan's beachhead.

The tide had gone out during the night and large areas of the reef near the shore were exposed. The receding waters also revealed the bloated bodies of Marines killed during the previous day's landings. Their corpses now added to the macabre scene of desolation on the reef. The sun was not yet high, but the dawn air was hot and humid and carried a sickening stench, the natural consequence of unburied dead in the tropics. The unforgettable odor was everywhere; the men on Betio were saturated with it; it clung to their clothing and filled their nostrils. And it reached out across the reef and provided an unpleasant foretaste of the island to the men of the 1st Battalion, 8th Marines.

The first wave of LCVPs grounded on the reef at 0615 hours and the infantrymen and assault engineers jumped off the ramps and spread out to begin a 500 yard walk to the shore. Along the beach the Americans who had made it in on D-Day turned to watch the grisly drama of others braving the defenders' fire. Japanese machine guns, never silent during the night, now increased their fire and the snipers holed up in the ship hulk opened up on the backs of the men trudging shoreward. Here and there a Marine dropped and another rushed to help him, often too late. A shell would explode and when the geyser of water fell back whole groups of lifeless figures bobbed in the area. Four waves of men kept coming in despite the heavy casualties, which seemed to the men on shore to be worse than those on D-Day. The enemy still held positions that covered the reef and hidden guns lashed out at the helpless targets without letup.

The Marine pack howitzers were able to stop some of this Japanese fire that was hitting the 1/8. During the night a bulldozer that had miraculously reached the island had thrown up an earth embankment to protect the five gun composite battery of the 1/10. Early in the morning, Rixey and his men moved two of the guns from the cover of this position to the right flank of Red 2 about 125 yards from two blockhouses on the beach boundary whose machine guns were hammering at the men on the reef. Disabled LVTs partially masked the line of sight to the enemy gunports, and Rixey personally sited the howitzers to take as much advantage as possible from the cover offered by the wrecked vehicles. At 0707 hours, using high explosive ammunition with delay fuses and minimum elevation, the gunners opened fire. The shells penetrated the embrasures and silenced the enemy guns temporarily, long enough to give the 1/8 a better chance to reach shore. Once this welcome task was finished, the howitzers were moved back to their main firing position and by 0800 hours all guns were ready to support the day's operations.

About this same time, Major Lawrence Hays, commanding officer of the 1/8, reported to Colonel Shoup for orders. About half of his battalion was now ashore, but it was badly disorganised by the punishment it had suffered. All flamethrowers, demolitions packs, and heavy weapons had been lost during the landing. Many of the men of the first waves had taken cover behind various wrecks and antiboat obstacles offshore, and these Marines continued to come in all morning, dashing for the beach whenever there appeared to be a let-up in the fury of Japanese fire. The heavy weapons equipment of the battalion and of the regimental and headquarters and service companies had not landed. Navy boat control officers stopped the fifth wave from going in to the reef so that carrier planes could attack the Japanese in the wrecked ship offshore.

The results of this aerial assault, which featured Hellcats strafing and bombing the wreck, were inconclusive. The fighter pilots could hit the ship with their wing guns but as bombardiers they left much to be desired. Most bombs exploded well away from the target, a condition that sometimes occurred ashore.

As the tide again shifted, the landing craft carrying the 37mm guns, 75mm half-tracks, jeeps, radios, and other heavy gear of the 8th Marines again headed in for the island. For the most part this time, the men and material came ashore along the pier, filtering in during the rest of the morning and the early afternoon. By 1400 hours, Colonel Hall had most of his headquarters and supporting elements ashore; there had been some losses, but nothing to approach the havoc wrought among the rifle companies of Hays' battalion.

Although Hall was senior to Shoup, he did not assume command once he was ashore. He considered that nothing would be gained by doing so, that Shoup was the officer that General Smith had chosen to lead the assault, and that under the circumstances prevailing on Betio the junior colonel 'was in a position to know more about what was going on ashore'. Instead, Hall made his communications equipment available to Shoup, giving him a more reliable means of reaching the division CP, and used the 8th Marines headquarters and service troops to assist in supply and evacuation operations. He dispatched his weapons sections to reinforce the front lines wherever they were needed. In view of the complicated minute-to-minute changes of the situation on Betio, Hall's decision was a wise one, as Shoup, and his omnipresent operations officer, Major Thomas Culhane, were probably the only individuals on the island who had an overall grasp of what was happening. Shoup's leadership, of necessity, was personal and he was deeply involved in every facet of the operation. And his exposure to danger was hardly less than that of many Marines on Betio, for snipers continually took his CP under fire and the bunker against which he had set his headquarters was still occupied by Japanese troops. Guards had to be set at the bunkers' entrances to check a sally by the occupants, who were eventually eliminated by a combination of demolitions and bulldozer.

While he could not make contact with Major Ryan, the reports Shoup received regarding progress on the western beachhead were encouraging. He was determined to link up the two groups of Marines. His orders to Major Hays were to take over the right flank of the beachhead, reorganise his battalion, and attack to establish contact with the 3/2. As the units of the 1/8 were fed into the positions facing the enemy strongpoints on the beach boundary, they relieved an odd assortment of Marines in many ways typical of the composite units that held the perimeters on the night of D-Day. Besides the handful of survivors of the 2/2, there were men from the 2nd Marines Headquarters and Service Company, Lieutenant Hawkins' Scout-Sniper Platoon, Major Schoettel's headquarters elements, and a group of amtrac crewmen whose LVTs lay wrecked on the reef and beach.

When the relief was effected, Lieutenant Hawkins was not with his men. He had joined Sergeant Bordelon in the ranks of posthumous Medal of Honor winners. Wounded by a Japanese mortar shell on D-Day, the scout leader had ignored the injury and helped to set night defenses on the right flank of Red 2. At dawn he led an assault on a Japanese emplacement bristling with five machine guns, crawling forward to fire point blank into the gun ports and using grenades to finish off the occupants. Wounded again in this attack, this time in the chest, he kept on fighting, destroying three more pillboxes before an enemy shellburst practically tore him apart. Even then, his indomitable spirit kept

Overleaf above: The sea wall, almost the only cover on the island from accurate Japanese gunfire. It gave the marines time for a breather before they went 'over the top' to take the airstrip. *Below:* While his comrades rest, a marine hurls a hand grenade from a hastily constructed entrenchment

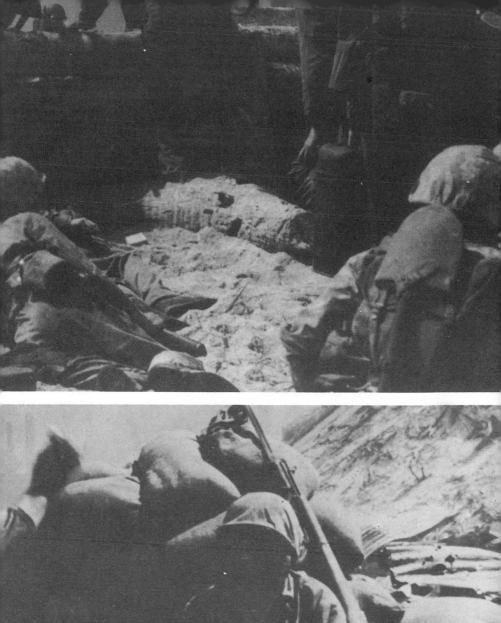

him alive for hours to the amazement of all who saw his multiple wounds.

Even with the efforts of men like Hawkins and his platoon, the Japanese positions on the western edge of Red 2 seemed as strong as ever when Major Hays was ready to launch his attack at noon. He had one medium tank to furnish support, but its 75mm gun and machine guns did not provide nearly enough firepower to make a dent in the enemy defenses. When the Marines of the 1/8 rose from the foxholes they had taken over, they were immediately driven to the ground by a surge of machine gun fire. Taking cover behind anything that offered some protection from this murderous fusillade, the men tried to move forward, timing their rushes with the blasts from the lone tank's cannon. Little was accomplished and the battalion, handicapped by the loss of its flamethrowers and demolitions during the landing, could not destroy any of the Japanese emplacements. A fruitless afternoon of heavy firing under the broiling sun came to an end at dusk with nothing to show for the day's efforts. As Hays' units dug in, they had to refuse their positions on the left flank and set up for all-around defense. The battalion was no longer tied in with the 2nd Marines. The nearest troops of Shoup's regiment were 250 yards away on the south shore of Betio.

During the night, the Japanese had plugged an apparent gap in their defensive patterns, the glaringly open western taxiway across which the Marines of the 1/2 had advanced on D-Day. Some elements of the 2/2, released from their positions on the right flank of Shoup's perimeter, had been able to cross the taxiway during the morning and join the units in the airfield triangle. But soon thereafter no one could cross the strip; enemy machine guns laid grazing fire across the open ground, firing down the long axis of the taxi way. It was sure death for any Marine to attempt the passage. Companies A and B of the 1/2 and some fifty to seventy-five men of the 2nd Battalion were effectively cut off from resupply or reinforcement. Their isolated situation, however, did not rule them out of Colonel Shoup's attack plan for 21st November.

The colonel intended to use the 1/2 and the 2/2 in an effort to drive across Betio and establish a foothold on the ocean shore. During the morning carrier aircraft were called in to soften up the Japanese defenses south of the airstrip, but bomb fragment and ricochetting bullets from this attack falling among the Marines in the triangle forced Shoup to call off the aerial preparation. Major Kyle had, meanwhile, taken steps to help his assault companies. He sent a platoon of ·30 caliber heavy machine guns to his right flank to reinforce Company C, which was trying to knock out the enemy guns that raked the taxiway. The ·30's were soon joined by a pair of ·50 caliber machine guns that members of the regimental weapons company had found on the beach. These heavier guns, manned by volunteer crews, chopped away at the Japanese positions with some apparent success, but Kyle was still unable to get across the taxi strip with Company C before the attack to the south was launched.

At 1300 hours, the 200-odd men in the triangle, led by the commanders of Companies A, B, and E, surged out of their holes and advanced onto the 200 foot wide airfield runway. If the Japanese had possessed inland defenses to match those they held along the coast, it is doubtful that anyone could have survived the dash across the open ground. As it was, the enemy fire was heavy but the casualties were surprizingly light. Once they had weathered the passage of the airstrip, the Marines moved through a tangle of undergrowth and shattered trees heavily pocked with bomb and shell holes to reach the ocean shore. Once they had reached their objective, steering clear of the mined beaches, the men occupied about 200 yards of the coastline taking cover in abandoned Japanese trenches. Strong and active enemy emplacements closed each flank of the new position. Almost as soon as the Marines arrived, they had to beat off a Japanese counterattack that came from eastern strongpoint. In this exchange of fire and grenades both sides lost heavily, and American ammunition supplies were

Right: **A captured Japanese Type 95 light tank**

84

A Japanese position identified: the
marines race forward to deal with it

With carbines, hand grenades, and machine gun ammunition ready, the marines work to prise the defenders out of their positions

seriously depleted. As usual, the field radios were faulty and no word of the situation on the south shore was reaching Shoup, Jordan, or Kyle.

When runners failed to arrive from the assault elements of his battalion that had taken part in the cross-island attack, Jordan reported his lack of contact to the combat team commander, Shoup ordered him to move his CP to the south shore position. About 1600 hours, the 2/2 commander and his headquarters group reached the isolated Marine units. Behind Jordan came a wire team from the 2d Marines CP and as soon as Shoup could reach him, he was ordered to try to link up with Major Crowe's battalion and block off the eastern end of the island. Once he had talked with the company commanders, Jordan called back to tell the colonel that there were less than 200 men in the position and that thirty of them were wounded, that they had little ammunition, grenades, food, or water left, and that the Japanese were opposing any move to the east in considerable strength. Under these circumstances, Shoup gave his permission to delay the attack until the next day and ordered the vitally-needed supplies sent across the island in LVTs, which were to bring back the wounded.

Major Kyle, meanwhile, had won the day-long battle with the Japanese

The Browning M2 .50 Machine Gun. A sturdy and reliable American weapon that saw widespread service during and after the war. *Weight:* 84 pounds with tripod. *Length:* 65 inches. *Rate of fire:* 560 rounds-per-minute. *Muzzle velocity:* 2,930 feet-per-second

machine guns for command of the taxistrip. The punishing fire of the heavy .50's finally decided the exchange late in the afternoon. With the enemy gunners either dead or driven off, Company C and its attached machine guns made a successful move in the gathering dusk to reach the ocean shore perimeter. Once Kyle reached Jordan's CP, the senior Marine, following Shoup's instructions, attached his men to the 1st Battalion and turned over command of the perimeter. By this stage in the operation, thirty-three hours after the landing, less than fifty men of the rifle companies of the 2nd Battalion, 2nd Marines could be accounted for. Most of the rest were dead or lying wounded in wards on board the transports.

The phone link with the north shore was severed shortly after Kyle took over, probably by enemy fire but possibly by the churning tracks of the

Right: **The wounded were ferried out on rubber boats**

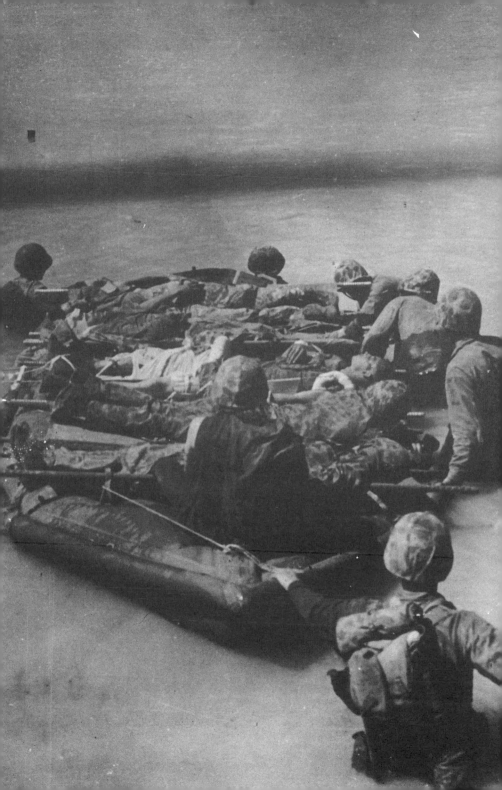

LVTs. Jordan took a couple of wire-men with him to relay the vital communication link when he left for the combat team's CP sometime after 1800 hours. When the 4th Division officer, now reverted to his original role as observer, reached Shoup's headquarters, he briefed the colonel on the situation to the south and brought him as well the means of contacting Kyle. Jordan had, in Shoup's words, 'done a fine job in the task he was assigned', a task thrust on him without warning in the hellish atmosphere of Red 2 on D-Day.

At the Burns-Philp pier, outposted by Major Crowe during the night of D-Day, the small outpost patrol had tangled with the Japanese all night. The enemy was obviously trying to reach positions where they could fire into the left flank of the 2/8. When the Marines pulled back in the morning, the short pier was covered by small arms fire and later a tank was sent up to blast the few persistent snipers that continued to plague the Marines.

Crowe's orders from Shoup for 21st November were to reduce the enemy position at the foot of the pier. Again Company F drew the unenviable job of trying to destroy the steel pillbox to its front and the large bunker to its right front. And again the mutually reinforcing fires of the two positions were too much for the Marines. Realising that his men on the beach were too exposed to the Japanese gunners, Crowe ordered them all off the sand strip. He sent a 37mm gun over to cover the north flank and prevent any enemy attempt at infiltration or counterattack.

The attempt to advance continued. A provisional platoon made up, like many on Betio, of Marines who had ended up on the wrong beach, filled in on the right of Company F. Its rifles added little punch to the attack. Even the addition of reinforcements from Company G did not shake the Marines loose. The lone medium tank that was available to the 2/8 did yeoman service, but it was not risked on solo missions ahead of the American lines. It found, in fact, its most profitable

The squad leader had identified another pillbox in the undergrowth

target behind those lines, when, during the afternoon, an enemy machine gun opened up from a supposedly cleared emplacement about 100 yards west of the big bunker. The Sherman blasted the gun port at close range, silencing the daring gunner, and a bulldozer was called upon to heap sand over the port and entrance, burying him.

To the right of Company F, the men of Company K of the 3/8 were pinned down whenever they attempted to advance to the east. Anyone who exposed his body was a certain stretcher case or slated for a burial detail's pick-up. But as surely as the Marines were stopped from attacking by Japanese fire, the enemy was prevented from moving anywhere within view by the accurate return fire. Battalion and company mortars pounded the area close to the American positions and the battery of pack howitzers on Red 2 vied with the destroyers and carrier planes for targets further east toward the tail of the island. An almost unending pall of dust and smoke masked the eastern portion of Betio, which was very slowly becoming the only part of the island where naval gunfire, air, and artillery could be employed with safety.

The elements of the 3/8 and Crowe's Company E in the airfield triangle made no attempt to move across the fire-swept airstrip on 21st November. Instead, the Marine commanders concentrated on resupplying and reequipping their men and conducted an unending hunt for reinforcements. All during the day individuals and small groups of men kept finding their way to the 2/8 and the 3/8 CPs to report. Most had spent the previous day and night serving with some other unit, but now they began to find their way home, concerned about their own outfits. As these men rejoined, the ranks of the depleted rifle companies of the 8th Marines were further increased by Majors Crowe and Ruud who stripped their own support companies and borrowed from regimental and divisional units to get additional infantrymen.

With fresh supplies, new stocks of ammunition and grenades, and the promise of more and heavier support on 22nd November, the outlook for the Marines on the eastern flank of Red 3 was brightening.

The most significant progress on 21st November was made by Major Ryan's composite battalion on the west end of Betio. During the night, a naval gunfire spotter, Second Lieutenant Thomas Greene, had gotten ashore in Ryan's beachhead with an intact and functioning radio. He gave the *ad hoc* 3/2 commander the means to make his plan of attack function to perfection.

In the south-west corner of Betio, the Japanese had constructed a heavily-fortified defensive position centered on two 5-inch guns in steel turrets and ringed by anti-boat and machine gun emplacements. Interspersed among these positions was a maze of trenches and rifle pits. Ryan wanted this strongpoint knocked out and Lieutenant Greene obliged him.

Temporarily interrupted as he issued the morning's attack order by a sortie of Japanese from a nearby 'safe' emplacement, an assault that quickly ended in the death of the attackers, Ryan cooly laid down his plan. Then Greene mounted the emplacement as an observation platform and began calling in naval gunfire. At 1100 hours one destroyer registered at Greene's direction and shortly thereafter a second ship chimed in. The noise was thunderous and encouraging, and the concentrated pattern of explosions was satisfying to the Marines, who had taken cover to avoid short rounds and the deadly hail of shell fragments. After ten minutes, Ryan signalled for an end to the firing, Greene relayed the word to the destroyers, and the riflemen rose along a hundred yard front. Almost without pause, the 3/2 methodically advanced down the length of Green Beach.

Enemy resistance was scattered and ineffective. The few times that a hard fight threatened, the two Shermans pacing the troops took care of it. One

tank, knocked out in the previous day's battle, had been repaired, and the other had been recovered from the reef and restored to working order with parts pirated from other cripples.

An hour after the attack was launched, the whole length of Green Beach was in American hands. Using the spotter's radio, Ryan passed the news to division of his success. He then turned his attention to strengthening his position by pushing inland to a point about 200 yards from the beach. The familiar teams of flamethrower operators, demolitions men, and riflemen were active everywhere to mop up bypassed defenses and to destroy the Japanese emplacements in the path of the limited advance to the east. A defensive line of mutually-supporting positions was established to hold the day's gains and secure the beach for further Marine landings.

While the entire western band of enemy coastal defenses had been readily overrun, the Japanese showed no lack of fight on both the north and south shores. Their defenses there were still well-manned and active. Ryan did not have enough men to attack along both coasts, but he did plan to try to reduce some troublesome strongpoints along Red 1 as soon as he consolidated his hold on Green Beach. General Smith, who considered the report of Ryan's victory 'the most cheering news of D-plus 1', was ready to commit the 6th Marines to provide the men and weapons to roll up the enemy defense along the south shore.

Since the afternoon of D-Day, the officers and men of the 6th Marines had been anxiously awaiting the call for them to land and help out at Tarawa. On board the transports standing off the lagoon entrance, any news of the fighting ashore rapidly passed from man to man. Maps of Betio and of the atoll were scanned for information about possible landing sites and Japanese defenses. The Marines lining the rails could see the clouds of sand and debris raised by air and naval bombardment and hear the confusing sounds of the battle being fought on the tiny island. From the ships' bridges, powerful glasses trained on Betio could pick up an occasional glimpse of the details of the fighting. The spectator role was frustrating

Reinforcement waves wait offshore

and the suspense ate at the Marines, making them edgy and eager to get ashore.

General Smith was no less anxious than his men to employ the 6th Marines where it could do the most good. He wanted definite information on the situation, however, before he committed any of the regiment's battalions. At 1022 hours, a message was sent to Colonel Shoup asking him if he had enough men to complete the job of taking the island. His answer was that the situation did not look good. Asked for a clarification of this report, Shoup replied at 1214 hours: 'Situation ashore uncertain. Colonel Carlson en route to division with picture of the situation.' About three-quarters of an hour earlier, Shoup had asked the division to land a battalion of the 6th on Red 2 to attack through the 2/8 and seize the eastern end of the island. The capture of Green Beach gave General Smith an alternative means of using the fresh regiment's power.

At a conference held on the *Maryland* on the morning of 21st November, Smith had discussed several missions that might be given the 6th Marines with the regimental commander, Colonel Maurice Holmes. Holmes im-

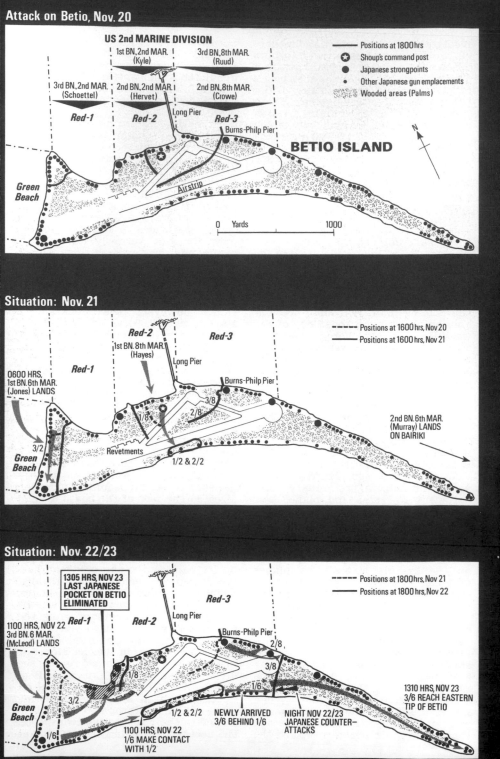

Attack on Betio, Nov. 20

US 2nd MARINE DIVISION

1st BN. 2nd MAR. (Kyle)   3rd BN. 8th MAR. (Ruud)

3rd BN. 2nd MAR. (Schoettel)   2nd BN. 2nd MAR. (Hervet)   2nd BN. 8th MAR. (Crowe)

Red-1   Red-2   Red-3

Long Pier   Burns-Philp Pier

Green Beach

BETIO ISLAND

Airstrip

— Positions at 1800 hrs
✪ Shoup's command post
● Japanese strongpoints
• Other Japanese gun emplacements
Wooded areas (Palms)

N

0   Yards   1000

Situation: Nov. 21

Red-2   Red-3

1st BN. 8th MAR. (Hayes)

Long Pier

Red-1   Burns-Philp Pier

0600 HRS, 1st BN. 6th MAR. (Jones) LANDS

3/8
1/8   2/8

3/2

Green Beach

Revetments   1/2 & 2/2

- - - - Positions at 1600 hrs, Nov 20
———— Positions at 1600 hrs, Nov 21

2nd BN. 6th MAR. (Murray) LANDS ON BAIRIKI

Situation: Nov. 22/23

1305 HRS, NOV 23 LAST JAPANESE POCKET ON BETIO ELIMINATED

Red-3

1100 HRS, NOV 22 3rd BN. 6 MAR. (McLeod) LANDS

Red-1   Red-2   Long Pier

1/8   Burns-Philp Pier   2/8

3/8

3/2   1/6

1/6

Green Beach

1/2 & 2/2

1100 HRS, NOV 22 1/6 MAKE CONTACT WITH 1/2

NEWLY ARRIVED 3/6 BEHIND 1/6

NIGHT NOV 22/23 JAPANESE COUNTER-ATTACKS

1310 HRS, NOV 23 3/6 REACH EASTERN TIP OF BETIO

- - - - Positions at 1800 hrs, Nov 21
———— Positions at 1800 hrs, Nov 22

mediately left the flagship and returned to his headquarters transport where he assembled his battalion commanders to outline the possibilities of their employment. While this conference was going on, a message was received from division ordering Holmes to land one of his battalions in rubber boats over the southern portion of Green Beach, to pass through the line held by the 3/2, and attack east along the south coast. He was also to boat another battalion, which would be prepared to land in close support of the attack. Major William Jones' 1st Battalion was given the rubber boat assignment, and Lieutenant-Colonel Raymond Murray's 2nd Battalion was detailed to the support job.

As the Marines of both battalions were preparing to disembark, the division received a message that changed the landing plan. Someone, presumably an observer on board one of the warships standing offshore, reported that Japanese troops were attempting to reach Bairiki, the island closest to Betio, by swimming and wading along the submerged sand spit that joined the two. Murray was ordered to land the 2/6 on Bairiki to block these escape attempts. Colonel Holmes then directed Lieutenant-Colonel Kenneth McLeod to embark his 3rd Battalion in boats to support either the landing on Betio or that on Bairiki, as required.

As it turned out, Murray's men needed no help. A preliminary bombardment by ships and planes was called down on Bairiki to help knock out any resistance. Then as the battalion's boats headed for the small island shortly before 1700 hours, a pair of Japanese machine guns opened fire on the assault waves. The planes orbiting overhead were ordered to strike again and try to destroy the enemy emplacement that was the source of the defending fire. One of the strafing fighters' rounds hit a can of gasoline in the bunker, and the entire fifteen man garrison perished in the resulting inferno of flame and exploding ammunition. When the Marines of the 2/6 waded ashore, they found no other Japanese, alive or dead. Murray had his men set up machine guns and mortars to cover the possible escape route from Betio's eastern tip and the battalion set up for all-round night defense. Murray's men and their rugged leader were both unhappy about the uneventful sideshow on Bairiki and the fact that they apparently were going to miss the main event.

Major Jones' Marines had the unusual task of landing in rubber boats, an experimental technique that had been tried in New Zealand as a means of crossing the reef off Tarawa. The transport, USS *Feland*, which carried Jones' battalion came in close to the reef off Green Beach about 1400 hours, the rubber craft were lowered into the water, and the men started to climb down the nets. Abruptly, the *Feland*'s commander was ordered to stand out further from the island and its dangerous reef. After all the boats were recovered, the ship moved out to sea but was later ordered in again; this time, however, the debarkation station was 12,000 yards from Betio. The long run in was made with LCVPs towing lines of six rubber boats crowded with men and equipment. Outboard motors, which had been tried in order to make the boats self-propelled, had proved unreliable, and the Marines had to paddle the rest of the way in to Green Beach when the reef was reached.

After the first wave had landed safely, the commanders ashore reported to Major Jones that the southern part of the beach was heavily mined. The battalion commander then directed the rest of the boats to land on the northern half. Emphasizing the wisdom of this decision was the loss of one of the 1/6's supply LVTs. It hit a powerful mine on the reef off the south beach, was split wide open and flipped on its back; only one crewman survived the explosion. The landing, which was completed by 1855 hours, was otherwise uneventful, and the 1/6 had the welcome honor of being the first infantry battalion to reach Betio without being shot up in the water.

At the same time the decision was made to commit Jones' unit, the division also ordered Company B of the 2nd Tank Battalion to land on Green Beach in support of the 1/6. Since all three platoons were bottom loaded in their respective transports, the necessary shifting of cargo to get at the light tanks took several hours. When the heavily-laden LCMs got to the reef, only one plattoon was able to find its way to the beach. Numerous potholes in the reef, a treacherous, shifting current, and a steep fall off on the inland side all added up to severe problems for the tankers. The company commander requested permission from division to land his remaining two platoons on Red 2 instead of Green Beach. His request was granted and he was told to move into the lagoon and land his tanks on the west side of the long pier. These lights came ashore all during the night and the next morning, joining two tanks from Company C's 2nd Platoon which had made it to Betio the previous evening. The rest of this platoon, which had been scheduled to go in with 3/2 on D-Day, was lost when its LCMs were sunk by enemy gunfire.

The one platoon of light tanks that did reach Green Beach reported to Major Jones about 1830 hours in time to take part in the attack he planned for 2000 hours. Once Colonel Shoup learned of the delay in the landing of the 1/6, however, he asked division to relay instructions to Jones to stand fast for the night and attack in the morning. The fresh battalion took up defensive positions behind Ryan's lines on the southern part of the beachhead.

Although the situation was confused and forbidding on the morning of 21st November, and Shoup's reports to division reflected this dim view, the news got better and better as the day wore on. In particular the supply situation was getting straightened out through the combined efforts of a number of Navy and Marine officers, including Lieutenant-Colonel Carlson. Carlson, who returned from the *Maryland* after carrying Shoup's report to Smith on D-Day, reached the reef off Red 2 in time to watch the assault companies of the 1/8 make their landing. Once he was able to find an LVT, he followed. En route to the beach he noted that a large stockpile of supplies had accumulated on the end of the pier and that a considerable number of men, who appeared to be trying to move this material to the beach, were pinned under the pier by enemy fire.

Once ashore Carlson reported to Shoup and was told that the ammunition and water resupply situation was still critical. Once again, Shoup asked Carlson to serve as his liaison officer to division and carry word of what was happening out to the *Maryland*. Carlson, of course, agreed and volunteered to do what he could to help organize the handling of supplies while he was on his way back to the flagship.

Early on 21st November, Captain Knowles, the transport group commander, had sent Captain John B. McGovern to the *Pursuit* to take charge of the ship-to-shore movement of supplies and centralize control of landing craft. In an attempt to achieve the same goal, the division shore party commander, Lieutenant Chester Salazar, and his operations officer, Major George Cooper, moved to the end of the pier where Carlson had noted the buildup of men and supplies. The pioneers of Salazar's own battalion, the 2/18, formed the backbone of most of the working parties that were handling resupply ashore and along the pier, while division service troops, aided by drafts from the assault battalions, provided the muscle to unload the ships and boats. One of the serious problems that had arisen on D-Day stemmed from the fact that shore party personnel were not used to handle supplies but had to be employed instead as infantrymen.

About noon, Carlson ran into Salazar at the end of the pier and informed him of Shoup's situation and needs. A plan was worked out to establish a false beach at the point where the reef and pier met and to have all the LCVPs unload here with the supplies being stacked on the pier itself. Engineers would repair the break caused by the fire on D-Day to make more of the pier available for use. Meanwhile all available LVTs would be rounded up and utilized in a shuttle service to the beach dumps on Red 2, where Salazar's men would handle further transfer to the troops ashore. Shoup would determine the

Overleaf: Mid-battle conference. Lieutenant-Colonel Carlson (seated), Colonel Edson and Lieutenant-Colonel Shoup work out plans on Shoup's map

**Classic fire-and-movement
operation against a pillbox**

priority in which supplies would be
landed. On the way out from Betio the
tractors would carry casualties for
transfer to ships' boats.

At various times during the first
twenty-four hours of the operation,
all or parts of this supply system had
been in effect, but there had been no
consistent pattern. Now all that was
needed to make it work was enough
LVTs. These Carlson got from Captain
McGovern when he visited the *Pursuit*
and explained the resupply plan.
The naval officer made eighteen
tractors available to the shore party.

From the *Pursuit* Carlson went on to
the *Maryland* where he reported to the
division Chief-of-Staff. Carlson's message had been overtaken by events
and Colonel Edson was able to pass on
the encouraging news that Green
Beach had been secured, that the 2nd
Marines had crossed the island, and
that the 6th Marines were ready to
land two battalions on Betio and one
on Bairiki. Preparations were also
being made to land the forward

echelon of the division command post
during the night.

Emphasizing the turn of events for
the better was the 2nd Combat Team's
daily situation report, which reached
the division CP at 1703 hours.

'Situation at 1600 hours. Our line runs
generally from the Burns-Philp pier
across the east end of the triangle
formed by the airfield, to the south
coast and along that coast inter-
mittently to a place opposite the west
end of the triangle; then from the
revetments north of the west end of
the main airstrip on to the north;
another line from the west of the
center of Red 1 across the end of the
island to the south coast west of the
end of the main strip. Some troops in
232 [target area designation] dishing
out Hell and catching Hell. Pack
howitzers in position and registered
for shooting on tail. Casualties: many.
Percentage dead: unknown. Combat
efficiency: we are winning. Shoup.'

The combat team commander's
reference to the pack howitzers readi-
ness to fire referred to all of the 1st
Battalion, 10th Marines. During the
day, Lieutenant-Colonel Rixey had

been able to get all of his batteries ashore. The gun crews had used rubber boats, life rafts, LVTs, any means they could come up with to get the other seven howitzers to the beach. Rixey set up one gun to cover the Japanese position at the junction of Red 1 and Red 2, and sited two others so that they could fire on the ship hulk and the various wrecked boats and tractors on the reef in order to discourage Japanese snipers from occupying them and harassing the Americans on the beaches. The rest of the 75s were laid on targets on the eastern end of the island.

The division had every intention of increasing the artillery support available to the Marines on Betio. As soon as Lieutenant-Colonel Murray reported that Bairiki was secure, Colonel Holmes was directed to land the artillery battalion, the 2/10, attached to his combat team on the island. At 0300 hours on 22nd November, the battalion began loading its howitzers into LCVPs, but an air alert stopped this effort. The lone Japanese bomber that caused this flurry dropped eight bombs on Betio, half in Marine lines

and half in Japanese territory. There were many profane and ribald comments regarding the pilot's impartiality as he flew north toward the Marshall's.

When the transports sailed away as a result the air raid, Battery E and a part of the headquarters of Lieutenant-Colonel George Shell's battalion were boated. These LCVPs headed for the island, leaving the rest of the battalion to come in when the transports returned. The boats arrived off the chosen beach at 0630 hours and as soon as its guns were ashore Battery E set up to fire. The fire direction center of the 1/10 on Betio helped register the howitzers, with the forward observer with the 2/8 adjusting the impact of the rounds while 'looking into their muzzles', an odd situation that had been anticipated and rehearsed in New Zealand. Battery F and the rest of Shell's Headquarters and Service Battery were ashore on Bairiki by noon. Battery D, which was originally scheduled to land on Green Beach in direct support of the 1/6, was diverted to Bairiki and landed during the afternoon.

D-Plus Two

The addition of another artillery battalion to the supporting arms available for the attack on 22nd November was matched by the arrival during the night and early morning of additional light tanks, some 75mm half-tracks, and more 37mm guns. A significant point in the operation was reached about midnight, when two jeeps towing 37s drove down the entire length of the pier. The Japanese opened fire on the daring drivers but somehow the pair made it to shore without injury to themselves or damage to the guns and 'prime movers'.

This increase in firepower, coupled with landing intact of the 1/6, gave the 2nd Division a chance to really put the pressure on the Japanese garrison. Two days of bitter and costly fighting had ensured that the Marines were on Betio to stay and now they had the means to end the battle. Colonel Edson arrived at Shoup's CP at 2030 hours on the 21st to lay plans for the next day's attack and to assume overall direction of operations ashore.

The first order of business was the arrangement of air and naval gunfire support. A fire control line was established across the island just east of the turning circle at the end of the main airstrip. The ships were asked to keep their shells beyond this line with the heavier guns of the battleships and cruisers concentrating on the eastern third of the island, at least 500 yards from the nearest Marine positions. Carrier air was to work over the same general area with bombs and strafing runs. The initial bombardment was scheduled for twenty minutes, beginning at 0700 hours. Then at 0830 hours, and again at 0930 hours and 1030 hours, the ships and planes would hit their targets areas again for twenty minute stretches.

The landing of the 3/6 was taken care of next. Lieutenant-Colonel McLeod's battalion had been boated since the previous afternoon and was waiting offshore for orders. Edson could reach the *Maryland* from Shoup's CP but was not in contact with any of the 6th Marines units. To reach them he had to have division relay a message to Colonel Holmes who in turn contacted his battalions. For the time being, Edson considered that the 1/6 should operate under Shoup's command until more units of the 6th Marines were ashore. He recommended this to General Smith and asked as well that 3/6 rendezvous off Green Beach at 0800 hours waiting orders to land on either half of the beach. Division passed on this set of instructions to McLeod at 0641 hours.

Edson issued his attack order for 22nd November at 0400 hours to the regimental commanders of the 2nd and 8th Marines. To ensure that Major Jones was informed of the plans, Edson directed Major Tompkins to proceed to Green Beach and deliver the message personally. The general scheme of maneuver fitted the disposition of the battalions on Betio. At daybreak, the 1/6 was to pass through the lines of the 3/2 and attack east down the south shore to link up with the 2nd Marines' battalions holding the coastal perimeter. At the same time, the 1/8 under Shoup's direction would attack west to eliminate the strongpoint at the Red 1 /Red 2 beach boundary. Colonel Hall's remaining two battalions, the 2/8 and the 3/8, would attack to the east, concentrating on the Japanese defenses at the foot of the Burns-Philp pier. The remainder of the 2nd Combat Team would support the attacking battalions with fire and continue to work on the Japanese defenses in the vicinity of their perimeters.

Ironically, as the blistering sun rose on 23rd November, the men on the Red beaches could see the water lapping against the sea wall. The tide had risen during the night and the water looked deep enough to float landing craft. Areas that had been bone dry since D-day were now submerged. The persistent and lethal strongpoint at the beach boundary discouraged any experiments; the wrecked amtracs and the bodies that floated in with the rising water offered mute and effective testimony of its strength.

Major Hays' companies were spread

out along a line about 300 yards long which stretched from the beach to the revetments at the west end of the airfield. The enemy positions in the revetment area and the center of the line were hidden in a shambles of twisted buildings, undergrowth, and shell-torn sand. On the right, however, the real Japanese strength lay. There concrete and steel emplacements girded by coconut logs and coral had withstood two days of desperate attacks. The enemy fire plan was so effective that no position could be attacked without moving into the fire lanes of flanking and support defenses.

Three light tanks of Company C were assigned to the 1/8 for the morning's assault and they tried desperately to knock out the pillboxes, often approaching to muzzle length of the gunports and entrances to fire. But the 37mm guns did not pack the punch to penetrate the emplacement's protective cover and the construction of the defenses' openings baffled efforts to kill the occupants. One tank was lost to a mine before the lights were ordered back to the 2nd Marines CP and two 75mm half-tracks were sent up to replace them. One of these was put out of action almost immediately when enemy fire damaged its radiator. In the afternoon's continuing attack, the firepower of the 75mm gun proved more effective against the enemy positions than that of the 37s. The half-track was more vulnerable than the tanks, however, and could not approach the emplacements as closely. The principal gains of the day were made by infantrymen and engineers who worked together to place TNT blocks, bangalore torpedoes, and shaped charges in position to collapse individual Japanese defenses. The battalion sorely missed the flamethrowers that had been lost during the landing. The searing tongue of flame and the billow of black smoke that accompanied each discharge offered particularly good protection for the demolition teams.

As a light trade wind heralded the approach of dusk, bringing with it the promise of some small relief from the day's smothering heat, the positions occupied by Companies A and C on the center and left of Hays' line were curved around the beach boundary strongpoint. Forward progress had not been great when measured in feet or yards, but a number of deadly defensive positions on the inland flank had been destroyed. Along the shore, Company B which faced the main defensive complex had not been able to make any significant advance, but its consistent pressure took effect on some Japanese nerves. Late in the afternoon a few of the enemy attempted to rush the Marine lines. They were easily driven back by men who welcomed the actual sight of a live target. When Hays' battalion dug in for the night it had succeeded in isolating the Japanese positions, cutting off the defenders from all contact with troops to the east.

Shortly after 0600 hours, as Major Tompkins was making his way to Green Beach with Edson's message, Major Jones was able to make radio contact with Shoup's CP and was filled in on the details of the attack plan. He was ordered to move out at 0800 hours, attack through the 3/2 to reach the ocean shore perimeter held by Kyle's men, and then to be prepared to continue the advance to the east on order. For his spearhead in the assault Jones had three light tanks with two in reserve. He had also prevailed upon Ryan to part with the only medium tank still in operating condition on Green Beach. About fifty yards behind the lead tanks, a platoon of infantry would move with the mission of driving off any mine-laden enemy who attempted to attack the armor. The battalion advanced on schedule in a column of companies with Company C in the lead on a narrow front only a hundred yards wide. All available assault engineers with flamethrowers and demolitions were attached to Company C to deal with enemy emplacements.

Surprizingly, the Japanese manning the ocean front defenses put up only token resistence to the advance of the 1/6. The sporadic fighting in no way resembled the grim struggles that had been waged elsewhere on the island during the past two days. With strong

Winkling out a stubborn enemy. A marine tries to pick off a Japanese defender in his pillbox

The patriotic Japanese

covering fire from the infantry, the light tanks were much more effective than they had been on the Red beaches. Their cannon and machine guns gave flamethrower and demolitions teams a chance to move close to some formidable emplacements and silence them. The enemy sailors appeared to have little heart for the struggle and the rapid advance of the Marines seemed to throw them off balance. Before the lead elements reached Kyle's perimeter at 1100 hours,

the 1/6 had killed almost 250 Japanese while suffering very light losses. Kyle's composite outfit had also had a profitable morning in local actions, killing about one hundred enemy.

Just about the time that Company C was entering the 2nd Marines' position, Jones received orders to report to Shoup's CP. There he was directed to pass through Kyle's position and continue the attack down the south shore at 1300 hours. He was to have one medium and seven light tanks to support his drive and naval gunfire and artillery on call. Across

the island, Colonel Hall's two battalions would attack in concert with the 1/6 to seal off the eastern end of Betio.

When the advance was continued at 1300 hours, Company A moved into the lead behind the tanks. The Japanese defenders became progressively more stubborn and the task of destroying them and their emplacements and bunkers harder and harder. The initial momentum of the attack carried the day, however, and when Jones held up his men as it grew dark, the battalion had reached a point near the end of the airfield's turning circle. Companies A and B established a night defensive line that reached from the beach to the edge of the airstrip. Company C moved across the open runway to the north shore and occupied positions that closed the gap between the airfield and the beach. The airfield itself was covered by machine gun fire. Crowe's and Ruud's battalions of the 8th Marines occupied back-up positions along the north shore behind Company C and guarded the open ground of the turning circle. Kyle's composite battalion of the 2nd Marines offered reinforcement poten-

tial to Jones' men on the south shore.

Before Major Crowe could make any appreciable progress on 22nd November he had to eliminate a trio of Japanese positions that had plagued the 2/8 since D-Day. One was the steel pillbox just inland of the Burns-Philp pier which had withstood persistent attacks by Company F and still spat machine gun fire at anyone who approached. The most prominent objective was the huge sand-covered bombproof bunker which loomed inland and to the south of the pillbox. A third obstacle was a coconut log emplacement in front of Company K whose accurate machine guns had succeeded in frustrating every attempt to knock it out. Each of these positions covered the others' front and flanks with fire and all had to be reduced if there was to be any advance.

Crowe made sure that all frontline units were resupplied with ammunition and rations. Lubricating oil was distributed and the men's weapons were taken apart and cleaned during the early morning. All of Company G was assembled to the rear of Company F to add weight to the attack, which Crowe intended to start on the left and then pick up all along the line. During these preparations, supporting mortars kept firing and at 0930 hours one shell finally penetrated the log emplacement in front of Company K and hit its ammunition supply. The resulting explosion blew the enemy position apart. At roughly the same time, a medium tank working forward of Company F's positions was able to slam several 75mm rounds into the steel pillbox. These two events enabled Companies F and K to move forward cautiously. As the Marines advanced the volume of fire from the huge bombproof and hidden defenses to its rear steadily increased.

The big sandy mound protected the Japanese in position behind it from Marine fire. All the enemy gunners had to do was to wait for the Marines to try to outflank the bunker and then they could cut them down, firing from defiladed positions at the east and south entrances and from emplacements and gun pits amid the rubble and vegetation to the east. The solution to the impasse lay in the seizure of the top of the bombproof, which would give the attackers command of the entrances and a good firing position to take on the defenses to the rear.

Assault engineers, led by Lieutenant Alexander Bonnyman, who was literally everywhere the fighting was hardest, led the attack. Infantry riflemen and machine gunners laid down a heavy volume of covering fire to aid the engineers. As they climbed up the shifting sand to secure the top, the Japanese almost immediately launched a desperate charge to drive the Americans off. It was Bonnyman who met the enemy head on, spraying the attackers with fire from a flame-thrower and killing three before he, himself, was shot down. For his gallantry and leadership, not only on this day but from D-Day onward, Bonnyman was awarded the Medal of Honor, the third man to win it on Betio and the third to win it post-humously.

Bonnyman and his men had been able to place demolition charges at the bunker's entrances and explode them. This fact plus the defeat of the furious counterattack seemed to cause the Japanese to lose all taste for the defense of the bunker. They began to come streaming out both entrances heading east. Those who tried the east entrance ran into a wall of small arms fire and grenade explosions; those attempting to flee from the south portal were hit by machine guns and 37mm cannister. Nearly one hundred of the enemy were killed within minutes.

After this breakthrough, Company E was committed and with Company G moved around the lagoon side of the smoking mound. Assault platoons from Company K drove forward on the

---

Above left: Holed up in a shell crater and taking cover behind blasted palm trees, the marines watch aircraft operating against Japanese positions. An LVT stands at the water's edge. *Below left:* Squad of dead Japanese, their bodies burned, mutilated and holed by bullets, wait for burial
Overleaf: The Japanese put up their strongest resistance in bomb-proof shelters, which could only be taken by hard hand to hand fighting

airfield side, pausing only to set off more demolitions at the south entrance. Guards were left to contain the Japanese still inside until a bulldozer arrived to heap sand deeply over the exits, burying some 150 enemy as a later count showed. Once the assault elements of the 2/8 linked up on the east side of the bunker, a general advance began. The Japanese no longer appeared to have any stomach for the hopeless fight, and as Crowe's men moved rapidly ahead, as many as ninety of the enemy committed suicide in their emplacements and trenches. The resistance from the rest was feeble and unorganized and did little to impede the Marines as they secured the area between the airfield and the lagoon.

To the left of Crowe's battalion, Companies I and L of the 3/8 in the airfield triangle kept pace with the forward progress on both flanks. When Major Ruud's men reached the point of the angle, with only the open field and turning circle ahead of them, they halted and dug in. Defensive positions were extended back about 400 yards along the south edge of the runway and the north edge of the taxiway to cover the ground so recently overrun by the 1/6 and the 2/8.

When Crowe's assault companies reached a point near the turning circle, he had them pull back because stray rounds from the 1/6's zone of action were whipping across their front. The major concentrated them on mopping up the area that the 2/8 had passed through so rapidly. When Company C of the 1/6 arrived on the north shore to take over the front line, Crowe placed Company K in support positions slightly to its rear and set up the rest of the battalion in all-round defenses further to the west.

After a seemingly interminable time spent waiting restlessly in their boats, the men of the 3rd Battalion, 6th Marines finally got a chance to set foot on Betio. At 0850 hours on the 22nd, Lieutenant-Colonel McLeod was ordered to land his outfit on the northern half of Green Beach, reorganize, and prepare to attack east when directed. The vast reef off western Betio and the shifting ocean currents caused many landing problems for the battalion and it was 1100 hours before the 3/6 was completely ashore. McLeod then formed a line with two companies forward and one in reserve behind the positions held by the 3/2. The fresh unit rested easy in the hot sun, listening to the sounds of battle to the east, and waiting for the word to move out.

The horrible smell of the dead, friend and foe, was thick in the air even though burial details were already at work using bulldozers to dig communal graves for the Japanese. The dead Marines, for the most part, were buried individually, many by their own friends who erected markers that showed their affection and sense of loss. At odd places throughout the battle area, these first crude tablets showed name, rank, serial number, often the man's unit, when these were known; just as often there a personal note: 'A Friend'; 'A Real Marine'.

McLeod did not get the word to advance until 1700 hours. As the 3/6 marched down the south shore, it traced the route followed by the 1/6 that morning. When he was about 600 yards from Jones' main position, McLeod was ordered to halt and establish a night defensive perimeter, remaining in close support of the 1/6. Before the night was out, things got so lively that support was needed.

On the morning of 22nd November, General Smith had decided to move his command post to Betio as the separate beachheads were merging into one. The value of the *Maryland* as a communication and coordination center for elements ashore but not in contact with each other had lessened. Ordering General Hermle to take his place on the flagship, the division commander, accompanied by the commander of the 10th Marines, Brigadier-General Thomas Bourke, the senior VAC observer, Brigadier-General James Underhill, and a ten-man CP group, boarded an LVT and headed for Betio. Landing first at Green Beach at 1155 hours, Smith inspected the men and positions of the 3/2 and the recently arrived 3/6. Convinced that he could best control operations from the

The cost. Chaplain Francis Kelly and assistant officiate at one of many funerals

centre of the island, Smith and his party reboarded the amtrac and headed around the beak of the island for Red 2 and Shoup's CP.

The enemy gunners in the beach boundary strongpoint proved to be no respectors of rank. They fired on the general's LVT, wounding the driver and disabling the vehicle. The CP group transferred to another tractor and managed to reach their destination without further incident. At 1335 hours, General Smith arrived at the 2nd Marines headquarters to be briefed by Edson and Shoup.

As the afternoon's attack progressed, the atmosphere in the command post remained grim despite advances that were almost spectacular when measured by progress on the previous two days. The whole tempo of the operation, the snail-like pace of the 'blowtorch and corkscrew' method of destroying the enemy and his defenses, and, above all, the heavy casualties the Marines had suffered, all combined to evoke an aura of resigned pessimism among the tired and tension-drained men. Smith's situation report at 1600 hours reflected the mood:

'Situation not favourable for rapid clean-up of Betio. Heavy casualties among officers make leadership problem difficult. Still strong organized resistence areas 212, 213, 214, 237, 210, 209, 208 (all near the east end of the airfield). Many emplacements intact on eastern end of the island. Present front line approximately on the western edge of 214, 236, and 212. In addition, many Japanese strongpoints to westward of our front lines within our position that have not been reduced. Progress slow and extremely costly. Complete occupation will take at least five days more. Naval and air bombardment a great help but does not take out emplacements.'

Three hours more of battle along both coasts had advanced the front lines further when General Smith

The 2nd Marine Division Command: Left to right, Brigadier-General Thomas E Bourke, commander of the Division's Artillery Regiment, Colonel Merritt A Edson, Chief of Staff of the 2nd Marine Division, and General Julian C Smith, Division Commander

called a commanders' conference early that evening. He and his staff were still convinced that a long fight lay ahead to secure eastern Betio. The general, who had assumed tactical control of operations ashore at 1900 hours, realigned his regiments and their missions.

Colonel Holmes was informed that all elements of the 6th Marines would revert to his control at 0600 hours on the 23rd. He was to continue the attack to the east with the 3/6 passing through the 1/6 to make assault. Murray's battalion would move from Bairiki to Betio, landing on Green Beach, and moving east to support the 3/6. Colonel Hall was directed to move the 2nd and 3rd Battalions of the 8th Marines to Bairiki to regroup and reorganize. Colonel Shoup's regiment, with the 1/8 attached, was given the job of eliminating the beach junction strongpoint and of mopping up along the ocean shore in the vicinity of the position held by the 1/2 and the 2/2.

As an indication of how serious the fight was expected to be, General Bourke was ordered to land the 4th Battalion, 10th Marines on Green Beach. As soon as they could be brought into action, its 105mm howitzers were expected to reinforce the fires of the two pack howitzer battalions. In addition to increased artillery support, a heavy preparation by air and naval gunfire would precede the 3/6's attack in the morning and the ships' guns and aircraft would be on call all day.

While these orders were being issued, the 1st Battalion, 6th Marines was hit by the first of a series of enemy attacks, a night-long ordeal that completely changed the outlook for the operation. According to Colonel Edson, the Japanese 'gave us very able assistance by trying to counterattack.'

About 1930 hours on 22nd November, a group of fifty enemy crept out of the dense brush in front of the defensive perimeters held by Companies A and B of the 1/6. Infiltrating the outpost line, the Japanese established themselves in a gap between the two company positions. Major Jones committed his battalion reserve, a small group of men from headquarters Company and the 81mm mortar platoon of Company D, to drive the infiltrators back. After an hour's confused fighting in the dark, much of it with rifles, bayonets, and grenades, the Japanese were either killed or forced to withdraw and the gap was closed. To reconstitute a reserve and to help guard against further counterattacks, Jones asked Kyle to place a company in a blocking position 100 yards behind the 1/6 lines. Kyle sent forty men from the 2/2 forward, a detachment that was shortly relieved by Company I of the 3/6.

Apparently the infiltration attempt was a probing attack which was to precede a stronger effort. As soon as the first contact was made, however, Jones called down artillery. Rixey's fire direction center responded with a crossfire from the 2/10 on Bairiki and the 1/10 on Betio. The pack howitzer shells were brought in as close as seventy-five yards to the 1/6's positions. Destroyer fire was directed at the tail of Betio and dropped to within 500 yards of the American lines. When the crescendo of firing finally tapered off to a steady pattern of interdiction and harassment, the Japanese knew little more about the location and strength of the Marine positions than they had when they first attacked. The fire discipline had been superb; few of the Marine automatic weapons had opened up and their location remained a problem to the enemy.

At 2300 hours a small force of Japanese appeared in the brush in front of Company A. Shouting loudly, thrashing about in the bushes, pitching grenades, and firing their rifles in the direction of the Americans. The enemy obviously was trying to create a diversion. Its purpose was to screen an attack by about fifty sailors on Company B's position, an assault that was quickly shattered by machine guns, 60mm mortars, and grenades. The enemy had been able to spot the extent of the company's defenses by their sacrificial charge and it was against these positions that the Japanese mounted their major assault.

Nothing happened for about four hours, while the Marines listened intently for sounds of an attack building to their front. Then about 0300 hours, several machine guns

The last of the fighting. Under a continuing pall of smoke, mainly from fuel dumps, the marines move inland

started firing on Company B and the right front of Company A, using some wrecked trucks about fifty yards from the lines as cover. American heavy machine guns were able to silence some of these weapons and the rest were knocked out by volunteers who crawled forward to hit them with grenades. The all-out attack, which everyone by now expected, followed the destruction of these guns by an hour.

Approximately 300 Japanese came boiling out of the brush, screaming and firing in a frenzied assault that hit all along the positions that the enemy machine guns had tried to tear up. The Marines of the 1/6 responded to the charge with everything they had – rifles, grenades, mortars, and machine guns – and knives and bayonets for the few Japanese who reached the American foxholes. Artillery fire was again brought to within 75 yards of the perimeter and the guns of the USS *Shroeder* and *Sigsbee* blasted possible approach routes to the battle front. The flashes of shellfire and the moonlight silhouetted the enemy troops and the Marines could hardly miss so many targets. Within an hour, the few survivors had melted away into the killing zone of artillery and naval gunfire.

Dawn's light showed that more than 200 enemy bodies lay in and around the Marines' positions. Further out, in the area plastered by artillery and naval gunfire, an additional 125 shell-torn corpses were discovered later in the day. Despite this frightful carnage, however, there were still at least 500 Japanese troops left on the tail of Betio.

The Atoll secured

The 2nd Battalion, 6th Marines was to have landed on Betio during the night to be available to support the morning's attack by McLeod's 3/6. A shortage of landing craft delayed this movement, however, and the supporting role fell temporarily to the exhausted men of Jones' battalion. As it happened, there was little need to commit these men.

For half an hour from 0700 hours, carrier planes pounded the eastern part of the 2,000 yards of the island that the Marines had not yet secured. Rixey's howitzers then took over the preparation for fifteen minutes before the destroyers had a quarter hour of uninterrupted shelling. While this was happening, McLeod sent Company I across the airfield, through the 2/8's positions, and up to the lines held by Company C of the 1/6 during the night. At the same time, Company L moved up to the area of the recent counterattack.

The attack got off on schedule at 0800 hours as the naval gunfire lifted. All available tanks, two mediums and seven lights, moved just forward of the advancing infantry. Demolition and flamethrower teams, including those from Jones' battalion, were in the forefront of the Marine skirmish line which stretched across the island. There was virtually no resistance for 200 yards as the Americans moved into what was probably the most shell-shattered area of Betio. Japanese bodies were scattered everywhere in the open, the victims of three days of ceaseless bombardment. Still more enemy dead were found in the maze of dugouts, trenches, bunkers, and buildings hidden in the thick vegetation. Most of these men were victims of their own refusal to surrender; they had shot themselves by triggering a rifle with a toe or clasped grenades to their bodies. Those that were alive were often listless and indifferent to the Marines' approach, offering no resis-

The western end of Betio. The woods and beaches bristle with gun emplacements, ranging from 8 inch naval guns to 13mm machine guns. The log barricade can be seen near the water's edge

Few defenders allowed themselves
to be taken alive

This Japanese preferred to die fighting

Most of the prisoners were Korean labourers

tance as the Shermans and flame-throwers blasted and seared their hideouts.

The first and only effective opposition to the morning's advance developed on the northern shore in an area dominated by several bunkers and pillboxes with open ground on its western approaches. Rather than lose the momentum of his attack, which

The fighting over, the marines have time to relax. For such conquests hundreds died

was in part responsible for the disorganized state of enemy resistance, McLeod left Company I to deal with the strongpoint. Company L passed around in heavy cover to the right and then spread out beyond across the island on a front 200 yards wide: Company K followed in support. By 1310 hours, after a short destroyer bombardment was called on the extreme tip of the island, the lead element of the battalion reached their objective.

During the swift morning's advance,

McLeod's men had killed or accounted for 475 Japanese and taken fourteen prisoners, mostly Koreans. The cost of this victory, most of it a result of Company I's struggle to reduce the strongpoint it had encountered, was nine Marines killed and twenty-five wounded. McLeod's own report of the action told the story of what happened:

'At no time was there any determined defensive. I did not use artillery at all and called for naval gunfire for only about five minutes, which was all the support used by me. We used flamethrowers and could have used more. Medium tanks were excellent. My light tanks didn't fire a shot.'

Apart from the Japanese remaining the eastern end of the island, the only sizeable body of enemy left on Betio on the morning of 23rd November was the defenders of the strongpoint on the Red beach boundary. The incredibly determined gun crews, hidden in well-concealed, well-sited, and well-constructed emplacements and bunkers, had withstood three days of attacks. They had played a large part

Admiral Hill inspects a captured gun

Time to clean weapons in the Pacific sun

in disrupting the landing of four battalions and, undoubtedly, had done more damage and inflicted more casulties than any other group of Japanese defenders. The reef off Red 1 and Red 2 was strewn with the shattered hulks of amtracs that had fallen victim to their accurate gunfire.

Colonel Shoup's plan for the fourth morning of battle called for the 1/8 to attack all along its curving front line with the main effort initially on the right. At the same time, Major Schoettel, who had rejoined his battalion on the 22nd, was to swing the right flank of the 3/2 around through the area west of the airfield to join the 1/8 and completely encircle the enemy pocket. Since all tanks were assigned to the eastern drive of the 3/6, half-tracks would carry the burden of close-in fire support for both battalions. To replace the flamethrowers it had lost during its landing, the 1/8 was sent those that had been used by the 2/8, which was scheduled to leave the island.

The key to the reduction of the pocket was the elimination of the shore defenses, by far the strongest positions in the complex. To aid in this task, Hays sent two half-tracks and a platoon of infantry out onto the reef to outflank the emplacements. Aided by the fire of these 75s, the assault companies of both battalions slowly ground ahead using flame and explosives to destroy each Japanese strongpoint. The silencing of the fires from a large concrete pillbox near the beach seemed to spell the end of effective resistance. At 1000 hours, forward elements of Hays' and Schoettel's units met in the airfield revetments and began driving north toward the beach.

After three hours of slow, careful, but steady advance from three sides, the two battalions completely occupied the now silent and smoking ruins. A few of the defenders surrendered and others committed suicide. Those that continued to fight were severely hampered by the break-up of the interlocking system of protective fires. Most emplacements were outflanked and taken from their blind sides. At 1305 hours, Shoup notified division that the pocket was overrun, its defenders dead.

As the morning's attack progressed without a hitch and it became apparent that most of the Japanese garrison had lost its will to fight, the atmosphere in the division CP brightened considerably. Reflecting the new optimism, General Smith sent a message to Admiral Hill at 1150 hours, saying:

'Decisive defeat of enemy counterattack last night destroyed bulk of hostile resistance. Expect complete annihilation of enemy on Betio this date. Strongly recommended that you and your chief-of-staff come ashore this date to get information about the type of hostile resistance which will be encountered in future operations.'

Within an hour, the admiral and some of his staff had landed on Betio, in time for General Smith's official declaration of the end of organized resistence. At 1330 hours, a long and bloody seventy-six hours after the first assault LVTs ground ashore, the island was captured. The victory signal sent to Admiral Spruance on the *Indianapolis* and to Admiral Turner and General Holland Smith on the *Pennsylvania* did not mean that all the garrison was dead or captured. Far from it. Mopping up action continued for several days on Betio as patrols checked and rechecked the multitude of burnt and shattered defenses. And there was still the rest of Tarawa to be secured. Scouts had discovered at least a hundred Japanese troops on Buota, a long slim island that formed the southeast angle of the atoll, and there was the possibility that there might be more.

All day long on Betio the relentless hunt for the enemy continued; few prisoners were taken. In the entire Tarawa campaign, only 146 of the defenders surrendered and all but seventeen of these were Koreans. Eighty-one of this total were taken from positions along Green Beach. The rest of the nearly 5,000-man garrison died fighting or killed themselves rather than face the disgrace and ostracism that surrender meant to the Japanese.

Two reinforcements took place on 23rd November, both too late to have any effect on the fighting. The first gun sections of Lieutenant-Colonel Kenneth A Jorgensen's 4th Battalion,

10th Marines arrived on Green Beach during the morning. The battalion commander himself helped wheel the first 105mm howitzer into firing position, but his eagerness to get into action was stymied by the rapid advance of the 3/6 which needed no artillery support to seize the tip of the island. Lieutenant-Colonel Murray's battalion also moved to Betio during the morning, but there was no need to employ it. Instead, the 6/2 was given the job of mopping up the rest of Tarawa Atoll, a task which it would start on 24th November.

Colonel Hall, using the boats that had brought Murray's unit to Betio, moved the survivors of the 2/8 and the 3/8 to Bairiki during the afternoon. Once the Marines were ashore on the neighboring island, a definitive roll call was held and the men were queried to account for as many of those missing in action as possible. When the final casualty lists of all 2nd Division elements were tabulated, there were still eighty-eight enlisted Marines missing, assuredly dead, but men whose deaths went unnoticed and whose bodies were never identified. This grim but necessary process was taking place on Betio also as the adjutants, sergeant-majors, and first sergeants of the various units tried to account for everyone on their muster rolls. This tally was not completed until the division left Tarawa and even then was not final, since the toll of dead climbed as some of the more seriously wounded died, and the number of wounded mounted as those who had ignored their wounds in the heat of battle showed up in hospitals and sick bays to be treated.

The division's action report showed that fifty-seven Marine officers, two Naval officers, and 925 enlisted men, twenty-seven of them Corpsmen of Seabees, had been killed in action. The wounded in action figures were ninety officers (two Naval), and 2,072 enlisted men (forty-nine Naval).

1,115 members of the 2nd Marine Division were lost in the seizure of Tarawa. The wounded who survived totalled 2,292. Since 16,692 Marines and 1,396 sailors participated in the assault and capture of the atoll, the overall casualty rate was 18.8 per cent of those engaged. For many

heavily committed units, such as the 2nd Amphibian Tractor Battalion, the percentage was much higher; the amtrac unit suffered 323 casualties, including the battalion commander, Major Henry Drewes, killed on D-Day, out of a total landing strength of 661 officers and men.

Well before the battle for Betio ended, the Seabees of Commander Lawrence Tull's 18th Naval Construction Battalion (3rd Battalion, 18th Marines) had begun landing their heavy equipment. The naval construction men's primary task was the rehabilitation of the airfield for American use, but, as was usual in the Pacific, the Seabees managed to get involved in the ground action also. Some of their bulldozers were called upon to help smother the enemy in his emplacements and many of the sailors participated in mopping up actions in and around the airfield. The dozers, graders, and trucks began working on the airfield's main runway on 22nd November when it was still swept by Japanese small arms fire. Shell holes were filled in and heaps of coral were smoothed down to provide a solid landing surface.

About noon on the 23rd, even before General Smith declared the island secure, a carrier plane swooped down, landed, and gunned its way through the construction equipment to a stop. The pilot was immediately surrounded by a curious crowd of Marines and Seabees, mainly interested in finding out if news of their epic battle was reaching home. Evidently whatever trouble had caused the pilot to land, if indeed he had any trouble, was soon righted as he took off again within an hour having taken the title of the first American pilot to land on Betio. The sight of a plane landing on the field they had fought so hard to capture made the battle seem more meaningful to many of the weary onlookers.

Orders for night defense on the 23rd called the infantry battalions to dig in all along the shore line to be prepared for the eventuality, however remote, that the enemy might attempt a counterlanding. Even with the screen of warships around the atoll, this had to be considered as a possibility. The enemy fleet at this stage of the war still posed a formidable threat to the Americans and there was no guarantee that a sortie from Truk would not be mounted. In any event, the 2nd Division had no intention of giving up what it had won.

The men dug in deeply, respecting the Japanese aircraft that had raided the island each night since the landing. The thought of surviving the holocaust of ground combat only to fall victim to an enemy bomb spurred the digging. It was well that the holes were deep. Shortly before dusk, a Marine pitched a thermite grenade into a dugout to take care of a Japanese holdout. The dugout proved to be

Demolition squads and infantry clear out the last of the defences

an underground magazine for 5-inch shells and the resulting explosions made life miserable for everyone on the eastern end of Betio. The shells blew up in turn, shooting off in all directions and scattering fragments all through the night. The Americans got a small taste of what it must have been like for the Japanese to exist through the naval gunfire bombardment. During the excitement, some enemy troops emerged from hiding places to strike a final blow. An officer in the 1/6 was killed and two enlisted Marines were bayoneted to death in their foxholes by these diehards.

In the morning the Marines could see a welcome sight in the lagoon. Their transports were standing

off shore. The long pier was put into operation as an exit route for Marines leaving Betio, as long lines of men snaked their way toward the pier head from all over the island. The bustle of activity seemed to emphasize the end of the fighting, but it did nothing to get rid of the smell of the thousands of enemy dead. Many of the combat veterans of the 2nd Marines turned aside from their files to throw up their morning's meal, overwhelmed by the stench. On Bairiki, the 8th Marines, happily away from the horrible odor, also started loading into ship's boats to leave Tarawa.

It was at this time that General Holland Smith arrived at Betio from Makin to see for himself the havoc wrought in the bitter struggle for control of the island. He and Julian Smith walked through the litter of battle, looking at the many emplacements that were relatively intact even after the flamethrower and demolition treatment. They watched the mop-up squads of engineers, pioneers, and infantrymen systematically search for enemy stragglers. All over the island there were the sounds of explosions as dugouts and bunkers were packed with charges strong enough to demolish the incredibly strong defenses that the Japanese had built – and died to hold.

At noon on 24th November, the two generals witnessed a formal flag-raising ceremony near the division CP. Two battered and stripped trunks

Above: Supplies, camouflaged against air retaliation, are brought across the beaches. *Below:* As the occupation troops move in, the marines march out

US Marine & Navy Personnel Casualties on Betio

Casualties suffered by Officers and Enlisted men in action   **(1 symbol=10 casualties)**

	UNITED STATES MARINE CORPS	US NAVY
Killed	🧍🧍🧍🧍🧍 51 officers 🧍🧍🧍🧍🧍🧍🧍🧍🧍🧍🧍🧍🧍🧍🧍🧍🧍🧍🧍🧍🧍🧍🧍🧍🧍🧍🧍🧍 🧍🧍🧍🧍🧍🧍🧍🧍🧍🧍🧍🧍🧍🧍🧍🧍🧍🧍🧍🧍🧍🧍🧍🧍🧍🧍🧍🧍 🧍🧍🧍🧍🧍🧍🧍🧍🧍🧍🧍🧍🧍🧍🧍🧍🧍🧍🧍🧍🧍🧍🧍🧍🧍🧍🧍🧍 🧍🧍🧍🧍🧍🧍🧍🧍🧍🧍 853 men	2 officers 🧍🧍🧍 28 men
Died of wounds	🧍 9 officers 🧍🧍🧍🧍🧍🧍🧍🧍 84 men	
Wounded	🧍🧍🧍🧍🧍🧍🧍🧍🧍🧍🧍 109 officers 🧍🧍🧍🧍🧍🧍🧍🧍🧍🧍🧍🧍🧍🧍🧍🧍🧍🧍🧍🧍🧍🧍🧍🧍🧍🧍🧍🧍🧍🧍🧍 🧍🧍🧍🧍🧍🧍🧍🧍🧍🧍🧍🧍🧍🧍🧍🧍🧍🧍🧍🧍🧍🧍🧍🧍🧍🧍🧍🧍🧍🧍🧍 🧍🧍🧍🧍🧍🧍🧍🧍🧍🧍🧍🧍🧍🧍🧍🧍🧍🧍🧍🧍🧍🧍🧍🧍🧍🧍🧍🧍🧍🧍🧍 🧍🧍🧍🧍🧍🧍🧍🧍🧍🧍🧍🧍🧍🧍🧍🧍🧍🧍🧍🧍🧍🧍🧍🧍🧍🧍🧍🧍🧍🧍🧍 🧍🧍🧍🧍🧍🧍🧍🧍🧍🧍🧍🧍🧍🧍🧍🧍🧍🧍🧍🧍🧍🧍🧍🧍🧍🧍🧍🧍🧍🧍🧍 🧍🧍🧍🧍🧍🧍🧍🧍🧍🧍🧍🧍🧍🧍🧍🧍🧍🧍🧍🧍🧍🧍🧍🧍🧍🧍🧍🧍🧍🧍🧍 🧍🧍🧍🧍🧍🧍🧍🧍🧍🧍🧍🧍🧍🧍🧍🧍🧍🧍🧍🧍🧍🧍🧍🧍🧍🧍🧍🧍🧍🧍🧍 🧍 2,124 men	2 officers 🧍🧍🧍🧍🧍🧍 57 men
Missing	🧍🧍🧍🧍🧍🧍🧍🧍🧍 88 men	

Casualties incurred by the Marines and the US Navy during the fight for Betio. The American public was shocked that such an apparently minor gain should have cost nearly 3,000 dead and wounded

The Stars and Stripes is run up on a palm tree

of palm trees served as the flagpoles. An American flag was run up one tree and a British Union Jack, borrowed from the flag locker of the *Monrovia* by the New Zealanders of Admiral Turner's 'Foreign Legion' was hauled up the other. As a Marine blew 'To the Colors', the notes of the bugle reached men all over the island and they straightened to attention. Those who were wearing helmets and caps saluted, following the naval custom. Tears ran unashamedly down many a dirty and tired face. To men who had fought for their country, and fought as hard as any Americans had ever fought, the simple respect for the flag was automatic and heartfelt.

The fall of Betio meant that the major task of the operation was over, but now the atoll itself had to be secured. There were still Japanese troops on the other islands, just how many no one was sure. The job of hunting down these remnants of the garrison was logically given to the 2nd Battalion, 6th Marines, the only

infantry battalion of the 2nd Division that had not taken part in the fighting.

The other islands of Tarawa Atoll had been checked to some extent by Company D of the 2nd Tank Battalion while the fighting on Betio was going on. The company was not a tank unit, but rather the division's reconnaissance element. On 21st November, a platoon of scouts landed on Eita, the island immediately east of Bairiki, and found it uninhabited but well stocked with dumps of bombs, mines, and fuel. On the same day, another platoon went ashore on Buota, the largest and longest island of the atoll. These scouts struck lucky, locating an enemy force they estimated at about a hundred men and a radio station near the elbow bend of the narrow strip of land. Far outnumbered by the Japanese unit, the Marines pulled out after nightfall.

On the 22nd, a scout platoon landed on an unnamed island about four miles north of Buota. These men picked up a few natives and captured an enemy laborer. The next night, the Japanese from Buota marched north up the atoll, bypassing the positions of the handful of silently watching Marines. Perhaps the activity on the neighboring island had convinced the enemy commander that it was time to move on. During the day on the 23rd, Lieutenant-Colonel Manley Curry's 3rd Battalion, 10th Marines had landed on Eita. The artillery unit's pack howitzers were supposed to have joined in the fires laid on Betio, but the end of the battle there gave them a new mission – support for the 2/6 in its sweep of the atoll.

At 0500 hours on 24th November, Murray's companies began loading into landing craft at Betio for a move across the lagoon to Buota. Landing at the west end of the island, the battalion began a brisk march to the east and then turned north when it reached the bend that marked the easternmost point of Tarawa. After bivouacking for the night, Murray's men continued their advance, wading across the sandbars and reefs that closely connected the myriad of small islands. The pace of advance was so swift that it was apparent that 3/10 would not be able to support the infantrymen from Eita or move often enough to keep up with them. Battery G was detached with its trucks and guns to join the 2/6's column.

On the 24th and 25th, the battalion made no contact with the enemy, but the Marines did discover a friendly and curious group of natives near the mission station at Taborio, about three-quarters of the way north to the atoll's last islands. The Gilbertese, and the French missionaries who were with them, confirmed the fact that the Japanese force had passed through to the north. It was late afternoon on the 26th before Murray reached the south end of Buariki, the last large island at the northwest point of Tarawa. As the rest of the battalion held up for the night, Company E was sent forward to try and locate the enemy force.

As the daylight was fading, Marine patrols threading their way through thick underbrush encountered a Japanese patrol. A flurry of rifle fire was exchanged and two Marines were wounded; several enemy sailors were seen to fall. Both sides then broke contact. In darkness, the Marines withdrew to Company E's perimeter and waited out the night, ignoring the scattered shots the Japanese sent their way.

As soon as it was light, Murray moved the rest of the battalion forward to join Company E and then advanced on the suspected enemy position with Companies E and F in assault. In short order, the Japanese were found; they were hidden in small groups in the brush, protected by rifle pits and fallen coconut logs. They were hard to see and held their fire until they were sure of an American target. In the first outburst of Japanese rifle and machine gun fire Company E was hard hit, losing many of its lead skirmishers. Murray immediately passed Company F through E to continue the attack and called on Battery G to fire a concentration to cover the movement. After this one salvo, the artillery had to fall silent. In the dense undergrowth, visibility was too poor and the fighting too close for anything but man-to-man combat.

All three rifle companies had to be thrown into the battle in a struggle reminiscent of the desperate clashes in the jungle on Guadalcanal. Rifles and grenades, and at times bayonets, were used to eliminate the Japanese who showed no sign of weakening. The fight raged for several hours before the main enemy position was overrun and the firing died away to sporadic outbursts as the Marines hunted down the few who had survived. By nightfall, the body count showed 175 Japanese had been killed; two Korean laborers were captured. The price paid by the 2/6 for its victory was heavy; thirty-two officers and men were killed, and fifty-nine were wounded.

On the morning of 28th November, Murray sent a patrol over to the tiny island Naa, about one hundred yards from Buariki and the northernmost land at Tarawa. The Marines found Naa unoccupied and returned. The battalion, its mission completed, returned to Eita to rest and reorganize after its march of thirty-five miles and the hard fight that marked its finish. One week after the 2nd Marine Division had landed on Betio, Tarawa Atoll was completely and firmly in American hands.

Makin and Apamama

Although Tarawa was the key objective of Galvanic, the simultaneous seizure of two other atolls in the Gilberts was very much a part of the overall concept of operations. The story of their capture deserves mention to set the victory at Tarawa in the context of the larger picture of American accomplishments.

At Makin Atoll the preliminary bombardment plan for 20th November was almost identical to that at Tarawa. Admiral Turner's escort carrier and gunfire support forces were almost as strong as those of Admiral Hill with the significant difference that more of the fast carrier task force was available. As he had planned, Turner was at the point of greatest risk to the success of the entire operation, one hundred miles closer to Truk, and ready to intercept the Japanese fleet if it sortied.

The prime target for General Ralph Smith's soldiers was Butaritari Island, which looked something like a badly bent golf putter with its head to the west and its narrow shaft, some six miles in length, stretching away to the north-east. The landing plan called for two battalions of the 165th Infantry to assault the western end of the island from the ocean, and for a third battalion to land later on D-Day morning on the lagoon side. Like the Marine landing at Betio, the Army assault would be spearheaded by LVTs to cope with the reefs that fringed Butaritari.

The men who manned the amphibian tractors were all from the 3rd Battalion, 105th Infantry, the reinforcing unit of Smith's landing force. Throughout most of the preparations for the operation, the general did not know whether he would get LVTs. As a consequence, he had the 165th Infantry take all its training in LCVPs, in order not to disrupt rehearsals. When fifty LVT(2)s did arrive thirteen days before they were scheduled to mount out for Makin, Smith assigned the

Easy going on Makin. The 2nd Battalion, 165th Infantry, wades ashore

3/105 the task of riding them in as the first assault wave.

Thirty-two amtracs made up the first wave off the western beaches: and the boat waves of the 1st and 3rd Battalions of the 165th followed. Unlike the landing at Betio, there was no lethal greeting from shore at Butaritari. The Japanese garrison of about 800 men, more than half of them laborers, was concentrated in an area about two miles from the beaches and it stayed in position. The tractor wave reached the shore at 0832 hours without mishap, but most of the landing craft that followed grounded on the reef, which was liberally studded with coral boulders and pocked by deep potholes. The soldiers found themselves wading ashore, but fortunately not through a hail of gunfire.

Very little opposition was encountered, only scattered sniper fire, as the battalions spread out to secure the western end of the island. Within an hour and a half after the landing, General Smith had a firm beachhead and the 1/165 was advancing east toward the Japanese defenses – a narrow belt of emplacements, trenches, and pillboxes that stretched across the island between two anti-tank ditches. As the Americans carefully picked their way through the heavy undergrowth that blanketed Butaritari, the volume and accuracy of enemy fire stepped up, but few of the defenders could be seen.

As this advance took place, the landing craft carrying the 2/165, preceded by a company of the 3/105 in sixteen tractors, moved through the lagoon entrance and turned toward the north shore of the island. The beaches chosen for this second landing led right into the heart of the Japanese defensive position, which fortunately was not oriented for shoreline defence. Preceded by a thunderous naval gunfire and air preparation which apparently dazed the defenders, the amtracs sped to shore with their machine guns firing to beat down anyone holding the beaches. There was almost no immediate response to this landing which took place at 1040

General Ralph Smith's 165th Infantry build up on a beachhead on Butaritari

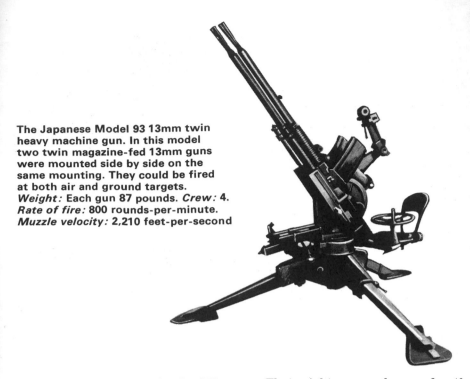

The Japanese Model 93 13mm twin heavy machine gun. In this model two twin magazine-fed 13mm guns were mounted side by side on the same mounting. They could be fired at both air and ground targets. *Weight:* Each gun 87 pounds. *Crew:* 4. *Rate of fire:* 800 rounds-per-minute. *Muzzle velocity:* 2,210 feet-per-second

hours, and the soldiers in the following waves of boats, who had to wade about 300 yards to shore, scrambled out of the water wet but unharmed. That was the end of the day's easy going.

The enemy had waited for the Americans to land and come within easy range of their hidden guns. Cast into the midst of the Japanese defenses, the men of the 2/165 spent a rough day in close combat with the deeply dug-in and well-protected sailors of the 3rd Japanese Special Base Force. The dense vegetation was made even more of an obstacle by the devastating effects of the preliminary bombardment, and it was hard to see the enemy emplacements, let alone destroy them. The same situation faced the 1/165 as it approached the western tank trap; visibility was poor and the Japanese held their fire until the soldiers were almost on top of them. The fighting was confused and trying for the Americans who were getting their taste of combat. As night fell, both assault battalions ending up digging in within grenade range of the Japanese.

That night was a horror for the untried soldiers. Enemy infiltrators made their life miserable, and the green troops responded to real and imagined attacks with heavy bursts of firing that at times seemed uncontrollable and were certainly wildly inaccurate. But the dawn came, and the men could see that little damage had been done except to themselves. They had learned a valuable lesson in fire discipline the hard way.

During 21st November, the battle continued at such close quarters that little use could be made of supporting arms. Instead, the fighting had to be left to the infantry and engineer assault teams. Slowly, but surely, these men did the job of destroying the enemy emplacements and killing their occupants. The western tank trap was crossed and both elements of the regiment joined forces in the punishing drive. The entire Japanese position was overrun by the end of the day; only the inevitable mopping up was left. The survivors of the garrison pulled out and retreated to the east during the night.

On the morning of the 22nd, the

The Colt .45 automatic pistol. A weapon normally carried by field officers and above, or by military police and other 'rear area' troops. *Weight:* 2½ pounds. *Length:* 8¾ inches. *Ammunition:* a magazine of 7 rounds. *Muzzle velocity:* 830 feet-per-second

The Thompson .45 sub machine gun. A light, close-quarter automatic weapon. *Weight:* 10 pounds 12 ounces. *Length:* 33¾ inches. *Ammunition:* one magazine of 20 to 30 rounds. *Rate of fire:* 600-725 rounds-per-minute. *Muzzle velocity:* 920 feet-per-second

3/105 crossed the eastern tank trap and moved into the dense growth pursuing the Japanese in a steady advance. Late in the afternoon, the assault companies were held up as they ran into a line of prepared defenses. After the battalion had dug in facing the Japanese position, it had to beat off a night-long succession of small-scale attacks, killing fifty-one of the enemy. At dawn only stragglers were left and the morning's advance to the tip of the island was swift and uncontested. At 1130 hours, two hours before the same type of signal was sent by General Julian Smith at Betio, Ralph Smith radioed to Admiral Turner: 'Makin taken.' The rest of the atoll had been secured without incident.

The cost to the 27th Infantry Division for the capture of Makin was sixty-six officers and men killed in action and 152 wounded, about three per cent of the assault troops. The cost to the Japanese was total annihilation. Only one Japanese sailor was captured, although 104 Korean laborers surrendered.

At sea off Makin, the Japanese were able to extract a far greater price for

the capture of the atoll than they had ashore. A Japanese submarine, the *I-175*, shadowed the flagship of a group of three escort carriers on the morning of 24th November. Enemy torpedoes struck home, setting off the bomb magazine of the *Liscombe Bay*, and the resulting explosion almost tore off the after part of the ship. Within twenty-three minutes, the broken and flaming hull slid under the waves. Lost with the carrier were the task group commander, Rear Admiral Henry Mullinix, fifty-two other officers, and 591 enlisted men.

The third atoll of the trio scheduled for seizure during Galvanic was Apamama, which was believed to be lightly held by the Japanese. Its lagoon, twelve miles long by five miles wide, was needed as the site of a forward naval base. Since little opposition was expected, only the VAC Reconnaissance Company, commanded by Captain James Jones, was detailed to make the initial landing. Jones' amphibious shipping was the transport submarine *Nautilus*.

After the sub picked up the company at Pearl Harbor, it went on to Tarawa

Support from the air forces.
Fighters strafe Japanese positions.
Right: Nautilus, the submarine
which delivered the reconnaissance
unit to Apamama

where it was to observe enemy ship movements. Then on 19th November, the *Nautilus* headed for its target, surfacing to make better time. While it was underway in this fashion it was spotted by the destroyer *Ringgold*, which had not received word that an American submarine was in the vicinity. In the midst of a salvo, a 5-inch round struck the sub and it dived rather than argue its identity. Once it was well away from the ships headed for Tarawa, the *Nautilus* surfaced, repaired the damage, and continued on to Apamama; it arrived

off the atoll on the afternoon of 20th November.

The reconnaissance men, riding a heavy current in rubber boats, made a landfall on the western part of the atoll's namesake island during the night. In the morning, the Marines started advancing east and then north along the chain of six islets that made up Apamama. They killed one member of a three-man enemy patrol they encountered, and followed the rest, running into a group of natives who told them that about twenty-five Japanese were dug in on the next islet. On 23rd November, an attempt to cross the sandspit that led to the enemy position was driven back by extremely heavy rifle and machine gun fire.

Jones decided to use his rubber

boats to move around the Japanese and hit them from the rear and asked the *Nautilus* to use its 5-inch gun to provide covering fire for the move. This strategem, tried on the 24th, failed, as the enemy troops kept firing despite the bombardment. Even the addition of the main battery fires of a destroyer which arrived during the afternoon failed to silence the Japanese guns, which by now had killed two Marines and wounded two others.

On the morning of 25th November, however, the Japanese position was strangely silent. Four men had been killed in the bombardment and the rest of the tiny garrison, eighteen sailors, had committed suicide. When Jones verified this news, originally brought to him by a friendly native, he immediately notified the occupation force that was on its way to reinforce his small outfit of less than eighty men and sieze the atoll.

On 24th November, General Julian Smith had directed his ADC, General Hermle, to lead a landing force organized around the 3rd Battalion, 6th Marines to take Apamama. The troop transport, escorted by the *Maryland* with Admiral Hill on board, left Tarawa at 1500 hours on 25th November and arrived off Apamama on the 26th. Hermle's force made an uneventful landing and set up defense ashore and then helped with the build-up of the base. On 4th December, General Hermle, at Admiral Hill's direction, turned over command to the senior Navy officer and with his Marines joined the general exodus of the 2nd Division from the Gilberts.

Goodbye Tarawa

The 2nd and 8th Marines left Tarawa for Hawaii almost as soon as the battle ended. As garrison troops and aviation units arrive in increasing numbers, the rest of the division began boarding ship and sailing for the division's new base camp, soon to be called Camp Tarawa. Most units had left by the end of November.

Only the 2/6 remained on 4th December, when General Julian Smith turned over command of the Tarawa area to the designated naval base commander. Murray's battalion stayed on for two more months to provide an infantry component to the garrison and then it too left the atoll for Hawaii.

By the time these last elements of the 2nd Division departed, the airfield that had cost so many lives to capture was bustling with fighters and bombers. Fittingly named Hawkins Field after the lieutenant who

had fought so valiantly on Betio, the air base was the source of almost daily raids on enemy bases in the Marshalls. On nearby Buota, a new field had been built from scratch and was operating; it was christened Mullinix Field in memory of the admiral who had gone down with the *Liscombe Bay*.

Two months after the battle, the whole aspect of Tarawa was changed. One place, however, was a constant reminder to the garrison of the cost of the land they now occupied. This was the 2nd Marine Division cemetery, a neat rectangle of white crosses enclosed by a low wall of coconut logs, an area of quiet and peace in the midst of preparations for war. The hundreds of men who lay buried there had placed a battle honor on the Marine Corps' colors that would stand with the greatest in American history.

The news of the casualties in the

General Julián Smith, Admiral Nimitz, and General Richardson (climbing the pillbox) inspect their conquest

battle for Tarawa hit the papers in the United States like a bombshell. Three thousand men dead or wounded in three days of fighting to take a tiny island that few people had ever heard of; it hardly seemed worth the price. When the correspondents who had landed on Betio filed their dispatches, the story seemed even grimmer as people read of men dying on the reef and in the waters offshore. Even the obvious heroism of the Marines of the 2nd Division could not shake the horror of the many who felt that this 'slaughter' might be the pattern of operations to come. For a time, the

The island is prepared for the coming drive across the Central Pacific Area

'bloody beaches of Tarawa' became a scare phrase of the editorial writers who attempted to analyse war strategy from their desks in city news rooms.

It took time for American opinion moulders to realize that the war could not be won without casualties. The foe in the Pacific was not overawed by American manufacturing superiority, nor was he cowed by the mounting odds against him in manpower and weapons. The Japanese had chosen to fight in a way that would exact the highest toll from their attackers. There was no cheap victory to be had in an amphibious assault against a well-defended objective. Observers were to learn that an amphibious operation was a terribly

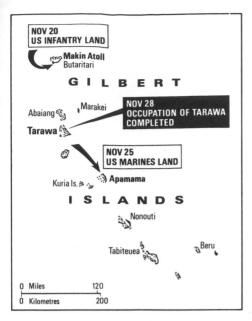

NOV 20
US INFANTRY LAND

Makin Atoll
Butaritari

G I L B E R T

Abaiang   Marakei
Tarawa

NOV 28
OCCUPATION OF TARAWA
COMPLETED

NOV 25
US MARINES LAND

Kuria Is.   Apamama

I S L A N D S

Nonouti

Tabiteuea   Beru

0 Miles   120
0 Kilometres   200

When Betio had finally been wrested from its stubborn defenders, it only remained to clear the other major Atolls in the Gilbert group, Makin and Apamama. This was done on November 20 and November 25

complex business, a business that could only pay dividends after costly trial and error. The body of doctrine that governed the actions at Tarawa had been laboriously formulated in the 1930's, much of it by men who now commanded the Navy and Marine forces in the Pacific. Tarawa firmly established the validity of that doctrine. Only combat experience – bitter experience for all concerned – could improve the techniques that confirmed the theory and practise.

It was no fluke that the operations in the Marshalls ten weeks after Galvanic were conducted with fewer casualties and in less time against similar targets. In a very real sense, the men who had died taking Betio Island had saved the lives of countless other Americans. The senior officers who led Galvanic drove their staffs hard from the moment the fighting ended in the Gilberts to find, dissect, and remedy every fault, in every category, that had been exposed. Seldom have men been so honestly self-critical and so dedicated to finding

error and providing solutions.

Those techniques that had worked well were improved. For instance, the value of the LVT as an assault vehicle had been vividly demonstrated, as had the need for heavier and better armor for the tractors. The reports from Pearl Harbor lent urgency to manufacturing schedules and vastly increased orders. From Tarawa onward, no assault landing took place in the Central Pacific that was not led by wave after wave of amtracs. In time, two and more battalions of tractors were assigned to land one division's troops, and amphibian tanks, armed at first with 37mm guns and then with 75s, led the troop carrying LVTs.

Naval gunfire spotting techniques were refined and thousands of practise rounds were slammed into Kahoolawe Island in Hawaii by ships reporting to the Pacific Fleet. Certain warships, in particular the older cruisers and battleships, became shore bombardment specialists. Naval officers were convinced by the results of the Tarawa bombardment that area fire was relatively ineffective against an enemy that could build fortifications as well as the Japanese. Saturation shelling was virtually abandoned in favor of pin-point destruction of individual targets; the length of preparatory fires was steadily lengthened and the weight of metal delivered increased correspondingly.

The success of carrier aircraft in controlling the skies over the Gilberts led directly to an accelerated schedule for future operations. The fast carrier forces provided Admiral Nimitz with the means to select and isolate any objective in the Central Pacific, even to hit an atoll in the center of a ring of Japanese airbases, like Kwajalein in the Marshalls. Improvement in methods and capabilities of close air support for troops was slow in coming, but steady progress was made, particularly in the area of ground-to-air communications.

The whole problem of radio communications was the subject of intensive study and experiments. Existing sets were waterproofed better, more and better batteries were procured and added to initial assault supplies, and orders for new equipment poured out of fleet headquarters. A new type of amphibious command ship, a converted transport packed with communication gear, was on hand in the Marshalls and the host of constructive criticisms and suggestions that grew out of experience in Galvanic provided a guide to its more effective use.

Techniques of controlling ship-to-shore movement in assault, reinforcement, and resupply stages were drastically refined. Clearer lines of responsibility were spelled out for both naval and troop commanders, and a greater degree of flexibility was built into landing plans. Ways to continue and improve fire support through the crucial moments before the assault waves hit the beach were worked out, so there would be no let-up in the rain of destruction falling on beach defenders as there had been at Betio.

In hundreds of ways, some big, some seemingly small, the naval and landing forces corrected mistakes, improved existing equipment, and sought better tools and techniques. Throughout the Pacific Ocean Areas, Nimitz's domain, the lessons learned in the Gilberts circulated. Troop training was intensified in tank-infantry tactic and in the use of flamethrowers and demolitions. The responsibilities of small unit leadership were hammered home. Ships. crews and landing craft coxswains practised unloading until the methods were second nature. In short, every phase of amphibious assault operations was examined in the light of Galvanic experience and the resulting refinement and improvement in techniques was increasingly evident as the war continued and its pace accelerated.

If there had been no assault on Tarawa, there would have been another fortress island where the painful lessons it taught would have been learned. The success of every subsequent operation in the Pacific owed a debt to the men who had died to take that tiny atoll and to the men who survived the battle to fight again.

Heroes were legion on Betio and the decorations that were won were richly deserved. Of the four Medal of Honor recipients only one, David Shoup, survived to have the Medal placed around his neck for 'conspicuous gallantry and intrepidity at the risk of his life above and beyond the call of duty.' Other men, like Michael Ryan, who was awarded the Navy Cross by his own country and the Distinguished Service Order by the British, reflected in their persons the courage and accomplishments of hundreds of other Marines. There was no way to single out every man who deserved an award. Instead, President Roosevelt paid tribute to all the Marines, Corpsmen, and Seabees of the 2nd Division in these words:

The President of the United States takes pleasure in presenting the Presidential Unit Citation to the Second Marine Division (Reinforced) consisting of Division Headquarters, Special Troops (including Company C, 1st Corps Medium Tank Battalion), Service Troops, 2nd 6th, 8th, 19th and 18th Marine Regiments in the Battle of Tarawa, as set forth in the following Citation:

'For outstanding performance in combat during the seizure and occupation of the Japanese-held Atoll of Tarawa, Gilbert Islands, November 20 to 24, 1943. Forced by treacherous coral reefs to disembark from their landing craft hundreds of yards off the beach, the Second Marine Division (Reinforced) became a highly vulnerable target for devastating Japanese fire. Dauntlessly advancing in spite of rapidly mounting losses, the Marines fought a gallant battle against crushing odds, clearing the limited beachheads of snipers and machine guns, reducing powerfully fortified enemy positions and completely annihilating the fanatically determined and strongly entrenched Japanese forces. By the successful occupation of Tarawa, the Second Marine Division (Reinforced) has provided our forces with highly strategic and important air and land bases from which to continue future operations against the enemy; by the valiant fighting spirit of these men, their heroic fortitude under punishing fire and their relentless perseverance in waging this epic battle in the Central Pacific, they have upheld the finest traditions of the United States Naval Service.'

Awards for gallantry: individual medals went to *(left to right)* Colonel Raphael Griffin, Lieutenant-Colonel Jesse Cook, Lieutenant-Colonel T J Colley, Lieutenant-Colonel Dixon Goen, Major Homer E Hire and Captain John O'Hara, Major-General Julian C Smith is at front

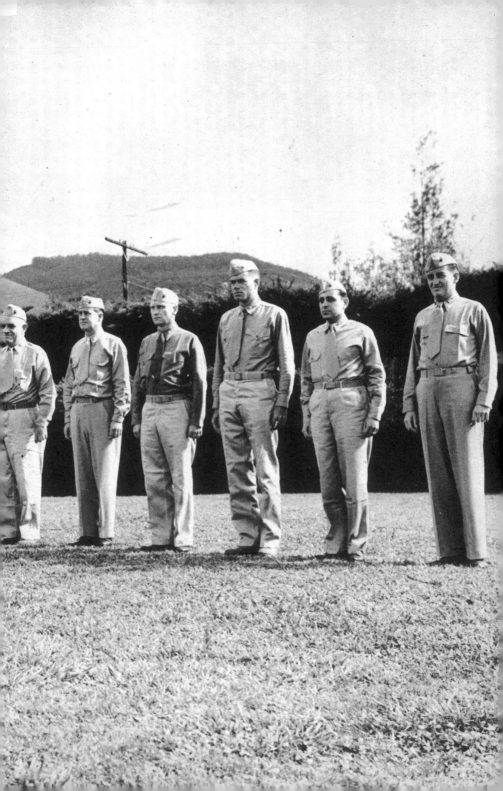

Bibliography

Seizure of the Gilberts and Marshalls: The War in the Pacific: United States Army in World War II Philip A Crowl and Edmund G Love (Office of the Chief of Military History, Department of the Army, Washington DC)

The US Marines and the Amphibious War Jeter A Isely and Philip A Crowl (Princeton University Press)

Follow Me: The Story of the Second Marine Division in World War II Richard W Johnston (Random House, New York)

Aleutians, Gilberts and Marshalls June 1942—April 1944: History of US Naval Operations in World War II Vol II (Little Brown & Co, Boston)

Volume 4, No 12, History of the Second World War, (Purnell, London)

Central Pacific Drive: History of US Marine Corps Operations in World War II Vol III Henry I Shaw Jr, Bernard C Nalty and Edwin T Turnbaldh (Historical Branch G 3 Division, Headquarters US Marine Corps, Washington DC)

Tarawa: The Story of a Battle Robert Sherrod (Duell, Sloan and Pearce, New York)

The Battle for Tarawa Captain James R Stockman USMC (Historical Section, Division of Public Information, Headquarters US Marine Corps, Washington DC)

Betio Beachhead: US Marines' Own Story of the Battle for Tarawa Captain Earl S Wilson USMCR *et al* (G P Putnam, New York)

Handbook on Japanese Military Forces (United States Army War Department, Washington)

Official records of units involved in the Galvanic Operation and correspondence and interviews with participants are all available in the Historical Archives, Headquarters US Marine Corps. Washington DC.